HEMINGWAY **&** BAILEY'S
BARTENDING GUIDE
TO GREAT AMERICAN WRITERS

HEMINGWAY & BAILEY'S BARTENDING GUIDE

TO

GREAT AMERICAN WRITERS

ILLUSTRATED BY EDWARD HEMINGWAY
WRITTEN BY MARK BAILEY

ALGONQUIN BOOKS OF CHAPEL HILL
2006

Published by
Algonquin Books of Chapel Hill
Post Office Box 2225
Chapel Hill, North Carolina 27515-2225

a division of
Workman Publishing
225 Varick Street
New York, New York 10014

Printed in China.

Published simultaneously in Canada by
Thomas Allen & Son Limited.

Consulting Bartenders: Sam Ross and Toby Maloney.
Researchers: Peggy Gormley, Tim Mackin, and Emily Schlesinger.

Design by Barbara Balch.

Library of Congress Cataloging-in-Publication Data
Hemingway, Edward
    Hemingway and Bailey's bartending guide to great American
  writers / illustrated by Edward Hemingway and written by Mark
  Bailey.
        p. cm.
      ISBN-13: 978-1-56512-482-0; ISBN-10: 1-56512-482-0
    1. Cocktails. 2. Bartending. 3. Authors, American. I. Bailey,
  Mark, 1968– II. Title.
    TX951.H26 2006
    641.8'74—dc22   2006045310

10 9 8 7 6 5 4 3 2 1
First Edition

"It has been my experience that folks who have no vices have very few virtues." —*Abraham Lincoln*

"If I had to live my life over, I'd live over a saloon." —*W. C. Fields*

Contents

Introduction

···

This book grew out of a simple observation: writers like to drink. Not all writers, of course, but most. Or at least they used to. The writers in this book, for example, forty-three great men and women of American letters. From James Agee to Thomas Wolfe, the list includes five Nobel Laureates and fifteen Pulitzer Prize winners, not to mention the National Book Award winners, Academy Award winners, and just plain best-sellers. It's a who's who of our nation's most accomplished novelists, short-story writers, poets, playwrights, journalists, and critics. And they all loved their liquor.

The two of us were talking about this one snowy night a few years ago. We were at a Christmas party in a bar in Greenwich Village, sitting on barstools drinking beers and feeling a touch nostalgic. The night had not started out that way. For any number of reasons (the cheer of the holiday season, the beauty of snow falling in New York, the pleasure of an open bar), we had been looking forward to a pretty serious bender. Yet to our surprise, the party was not with us. There we were, in a bar filled with writers, and the crowd could not have been more tame.

In the good old days, we imagined, things would have been very different. In the good old days, the myth of the hard-drinking writer was not just a myth. But clearly that world had disappeared long ago. Still, the stories remained—F. Scott and Zelda Fitzgerald showing up at parties in their pajamas, Ernest Hemingway busting John O'Hara's walking stick over his own head, John Steinbeck and Robert Benchley diving for wine bottles at the bottom of a pool. The drunken tales of wilder times. And, of course, the cocktails survived too, if barely—the Sidecar, the Stinger, the French 75—like the language of a lost civilization. We ordered more beers. But wasn't that at least something— the stories, the cocktails? We took another sip. And wouldn't it be something greater still to travel back, even if only in spirit?

We decided to give it a try. One more round, but this time a Mojito, as Hemingway would have had it. And a Gin Rickey for Fitzgerald. We watched the bartender line up the glasses.

....

In New York, Los Angeles, Paris, at places like the "21" Club, the Musso & Frank Grill, and the Ritz Hotel, classic writers drank classic cocktails. Some had clear favorites. Others were more fickle. What they shared, though, was a common thirst and a high regard for the well-made drink.

Through research, deduction, and a little imagination, we have tried to honor that with our own recipes. We have tested every cocktail in this book—tested and re-tested. They are well-made drinks, true to the spirit of their day and, as important, delicious too.

When asked about writers and their affinity for alcohol, Truman Capote quoted Irish playwright Brendan Behan, "We are drinkers with writing problems." It was a confession of sorts, that the scales had tipped for him. Maybe they tipped for other writers in this book too. Why did they drink so much? Did alcohol help or hurt their writing? These are worthwhile questions and there are no easy answers. But then this is, after all, a bartending guide, and who are we to say.

What we have done is to offer up some brief excerpts from their literary works. Tidbits from the novels and short stories, the plays and poems and articles that made these writers great. One thing is clear: however pickled these writers may have been, they left an extraordinary body of literature behind for us.

So let's lift the first glass to them, to these forty-three great men and women. It is our hope that through their drinks, their stories, their colorful faces, that you too will be able to travel back—to the good old days. All we ask is that you be a little careful as you go. Remember, a couple of cocktails doesn't make you a drunk, and no amount of liquor can make you a writer.

Edward Hemingway & Mark Bailey

UTENSILS

Mixing Glass   *Standard Shaker*   *Boston Shaker*   *Hawthorne Strainer*

Bar Spoon   *Measuring Cup*   *Jigger*   *Citrus Stripper*   *Muddler*

SIMPLE SYRUP

1 cup granulated sugar   1 cup water

(One-to-one ratio, as much as desired for use or storage.)

Stir 1 cup of granulated sugar and 1 cup of water in a saucepan over medium heat. Bring to a light boil and then let simmer until sugar is completely dissolved. remove pan from heat, and let cool.

   If storing, pour cooled syrup into a glass bottle or jar, cap tightly, and refrigerate. Should keep for a week.

GLASSES

Cocktail Glass

Highball Glass

Collins Glass

Old-Fashioned Glass

Double Old-Fashioned Glass

Champagne Flute

White Wine Glass

Pint Glass

Beer Mug

Shot Glass

GARNISHES

Twist

Wheel

Slice

Wedge

Cherries

Mint Sprig

Olives

Cocktail Onions

Sugar Cubes

Umbrella

HEMINGWAY & BAILEY'S
BARTENDING GUIDE
TO GREAT AMERICAN WRITERS

> ## "After one drink it's very hard not to take another, and after three it is even harder not to take three more."

A gee, often quiet and despairing when sober, was transformed by alcohol. The life of the party, no, but he could be terrifically entertaining. Director John Huston found that the more Agee drank the more he talked, and the funnier he got. A clever parodist, he liked to mime a piss-drunk Ulysses S. Grant accepting the sword from Robert E. Lee at Appomattox and sliding onto the floor. Although not an actor, Agee occasionally cast himself in bit roles. He played a drunk in both *The Bride Comes to Yellow Sky* and a television film on Abraham Lincoln. Clearly, he knew how to play to his strengths.

....

1909–1955. Novelist, journalist, screenwriter, film critic, and poet. *Let Us Now Praise Famous Men*, poorly received at the time of publication, is Agee's most celebrated work. His unfinished autobiographical novel, *A Death in the Family*, won the Pulitzer Prize. *The African Queen*, written with John Huston, was nominated for an Academy Award.

WHISKEY SOUR

Like many southern writers, Agee (born in Knoxville, Tennessee) loved his bourbon. One of America's oldest cocktails, the venerable Whiskey Sour is a fine way to imbibe yours. When made just right, a balance between sweet and sour is achieved.

2 oz. bourbon, rye, or blended whiskey	**¾ oz. lemon juice**
¾ oz. simple syrup	**Orange or lemon slice**
	Maraschino cherry

Pour all ingredients into a cocktail shaker filled with ice cubes. Shake well. Strain into a chilled cocktail glass. Garnish with orange or lemon slice and cherry. Traditionally, a raw egg white is added to give the drink a silky consistency.

The Whiskey Sour can also be served on the rocks in an Old-Fashioned glass.

From *A Death in the Family*, 1938

"BLESS YOU, PAPA."

"Rats. Drink your drink."

She drank deeply and shuddered.

"Take all you can without getting drunk," he said. "I wouldn't give a whoop if you got blind drunk, best thing you could do. But you've got tomorrow to reckon with." And tomorrow and tomorrow.

"It doesn't seem to have any effect," she said, her voice still liquid. "The only times I drank before I had a terribly weak head, just one drink was enough to make me absolutely squiffy. But now it doesn't seem to have any effect in the slightest." She drank some more.

"Good," he said. "That can happen."

"A poet without alcohol is no real poet."

One evening at a pub in England, Aiken and Malcolm Lowry (a writer who also liked his liquor) set to drinking at a relatively brisk pace. After more than a couple, they headed out into the thick fog. At nine o'clock, Aiken's worried wife, Clarissa, was stunned to see two mud-soaked zombies lurch into the house. It turned out they had staged an impromptu javelin-throw—this across an inlet where three rivers converged. Unfortunately, Aiken forgot to let go of the javelin and fell into the river. Lowry slipped in after him. Given the dark night and the slimy wall, they were lucky the tide proved lower than their blood alcohol levels.

....

1889–1973. Poet, short-story writer, and novelist. Aiken gained recognition with his first book of verse, *Earth Triumphant.* His *Selected Poems* was awarded a Pulitzer Prize, his *Collected Poems* a National Book Award. Aiken's best-known short story is "Silent Snow, Silent Secret."

NEGRONI

The Negroni, supposedly named after a bar-hopping Italian count, has a remarkable red-orange color and a taste as distinctive and complex as any Aiken poem. You have to appreciate Campari, and not everyone does. Like a Martini, a Negroni can be made dry or sweet.

1 oz. gin　　　　**1 oz. Campari**
1 oz. sweet vermouth　　**Orange twist**

Pour all ingredients into an Old-Fashioned glass filled with ice cubes. Stir gently. Garnish with orange twist. Sometimes a splash of club soda is added.

    The Negroni can also be served straight up in a cocktail glass.

From "Punch the Immortal Liar," 1921

Punch in a beer-house, drinking beer,

Booms with his voice so that all may hear,

Bangs on the table with a red-haired fist,

Writhes in his chair with a hump-backed twist,

Leers at his huge nose, in the glass,

And then proclaims in a voice of brass:

Let all who would prosper and be free

Mark my words and listen to me!

Call me a hunchback? call me a clown?

I turned the universe upside down!

And where is the law or love or chain

That can't be broken by nerve or brain?

Sherwood Anderson

> "When you get drunk there is no difference between you and a lot of drunken advertising men."

In New Orleans, an introduction was arranged between Anderson and the young William Faulkner. They became instant friends. As impressed as Anderson was with Faulkner's talent, he was equally impressed with his astonishing tolerance for alcohol. Faulkner attributed his own heavy drinking to his limp and a metal plate in his head, World War I injuries received as a pilot in the Canadian Flying Corps. Believing the tale, Anderson worked the details into a short story, not knowing Faulkner had in truth been too short to enlist. Years later, Anderson himself would be severely injured, fatally in fact. This was not due to wartime exploits, but from drinking itself. Aboard an ocean liner bound for Brazil, Anderson accidentally swallowed a toothpick at a cocktail party. He died shortly afterward of peritonitis—an infection of the stomach.

....

1876–1941. Short-story writer and novelist. Most famous for *Winesburg, Ohio*, a collection of interrelated short stories. In form and subject matter, Anderson's work was a major influence on younger American writers, including Faulkner, Hemingway, Steinbeck, and Wolfe.

OLD-FASHIONED

You would think with a name like "Old-Fashioned" the recipe would be set in stone, but in fact a heated debate rages around the fruit. Some argue to muddle it; others add it as garnish; still others leave it out altogether. It is not known how Anderson took his Old-Fashioned, but we like our fruit as garnish—and, out of respect for the author, no toothpick.

1 cube of sugar	1 dash simple syrup
3 dashes Angostura bitters	1 orange slice
2½ oz. bourbon, rye, or	1 maraschino cherry
blended whiskey	Lemon twist

Place a sugar cube at the bottom of an Old-Fashioned glass. Add bitters, and muddle. Pour in whiskey and a dash of simple syrup. Fill the glass with ice cubes, and stir gently. Garnish with lemon twist, orange slice, and cherry. Sometimes a splash of club soda is added.

From *Winesburg, Ohio*, 1919

ONE NIGHT TOM FOSTER GOT DRUNK. That came about in a curious way. He never had been drunk before, and indeed in all his life had never taken a drink of anything intoxicating, but he felt he needed to be drunk that one time and so went and did it. . . .

Tom got drunk sitting on a bank of new grass beside the road about a mile north of town. Before him was a white road and at his back an apple orchard in full bloom. He took a drink out of the bottle and then lay down on the grass. . . .

"It was good to be drunk," Tom Foster said. "It taught me something. I won't have to do it again."

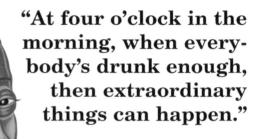

"At four o'clock in the morning, when everybody's drunk enough, then extraordinary things can happen."

In Paris, Baldwin spent many long nights in cafés drinking and arguing with writers James Jones and William Styron, fellow expatriates with a similar fondness for booze. At Jones's home, where they would often start out and end up, Jones had a bar made out of an old church pulpit. Late at night, Baldwin, who in his youth had been a preacher, would entertain his friends by delivering mock sermons on the evils of drink.

....

1924–1987. Novelist, essayist, short-story writer, and playwright. Best known for his autobiographical first novel, *Go Tell It on the Mountain*. Baldwin's second novel, *Giovanni's Room*, explored homosexuality and created controversy. An active voice in the civil rights movement, he followed with *Another Country* and *The Fire Next Time*. Baldwin spent much of his career as an expatriate in Paris.

SHANDY GAFF

In his novel *Tell Me How Long the Train's Been Gone*, Baldwin's young protagonist Leo takes one of his first drinks ever— whiskey with ginger ale. The Shandy Gaff is beer with ginger ale. Originally created in Great Britain, Shandies have been around since the late 1800s.

8 oz. lager beer or   **8 oz. ginger ale soda**
amber ale

Pour beer into a chilled beer mug, add ginger ale.

From *Tell Me How Long the Train's Been Gone*, 1968

OUR MOTHER RETURNED AND SHE POURED the drinks. I wasn't really permitted to drink, and, luckily, in those days, I didn't like to drink; but this prohibition, like all of my parents' prohibitions, was rendered a dead letter by the fact that my parents knew very well that I did whatever I wished, outside. Now, my mother said, "I'm making yours real weak, Leo," and handed me a glass of ginger ale only very faintly colored by whiskey. "That's just so you can feel part of the family," she said, and handed drinks to my father and Caleb and sat down. Caleb and our father looked at each other, but neither of them smiled. I drank my ginger ale. I thought of a girl I knew. I tried to think of everything but the room I was in, and the people I was with.

Djuna Barnes

"I've wrestled with tigers until my nightdress was soaking wet, that is, struggling not to take a drink."

Sharp-tongued and independent-minded, Barnes was a fixture on the Left Bank and a force to be reckoned with. Peggy Guggenheim claimed she averaged a bottle of whiskey a day. Walter Winchell said he saw her hit a spittoon from thirty feet away. Barnes enjoyed her lovers too, men and women alike. She must have packed in more than enough during her nights at Le Dome, Hotel Jacob, and the Dingo, because when she returned to the States, she spent the next forty-odd years as a recluse. Even a drunk Carson McCullers, who'd come around to pay homage at Barnes's West Village apartment, was left to cry on the doorstep.

....

1892–1982. Playwright, journalist, novelist, illustrator, and short-story writer. Openly gay, Barnes was a key figure in 1920s and 1930s bohemian Paris. Her second novel, *Nightwood*, with an introduction by T. S. Eliot, was noted both for its structure and candid portrayal of lesbianism. The book is considered Barnes's masterpiece.

FRENCH 75

Popular in Paris between the wars, the French 75 was named after the World War I French-made 75mm howitzer. These were the years Barnes was living and drinking on the Left Bank and, from all accounts, a real pistol herself.

2 oz. gin	**Top with champagne**
¾ oz. lemon juice	**Lemon twist**
¾ oz. simple syrup	

Pour gin, lemon, and simple syrup into a cocktail shaker filled with ice cubes. Shake well. Strain into a Collins glass filled with ice cubes. Top with champagne. Garnish with lemon twist. Often cognac is used instead of gin.

From *Nightwood*, 1937

"SHE BEGAN RUNNING AFTER ME. I kept on walking. I was cold, and I was not miserable any more. She caught me by the shoulder and went against me, grinning. She stumbled and I held her, and she said, seeing a poor wretched beggar of a whore, 'Give her some money, all of it!' She threw the francs into the street and bent down over the filthy baggage and began stroking her hair, gray with the dust of years, saying, 'They are all God-forsaken, and you most of all, because they don't want you to have your happiness. They don't want you to drink. Well, here, drink! I give you money and permission.'"

Robert Benchley

"Drinking makes such fools of people, and people are such fools to begin with, that it's compounding a felony."

Initially a supporter of Prohibition, Benchley did not have his first drink until he was thirty-one. This was at Tony Soma's, in the company of Zelda and F. Scott Fitzgerald, Dorothy Parker, and Robert Sherwood. Decades (and countless drinks) later, Benchley and Fitzgerald found themselves together one afternoon at Benchley's bungalow in Hollywood. Checking his watch, Benchley noticed that it was five o'clock and that the "small wagon" he was then on allowed for drinks after five. He insisted on stirring up a pitcher of cocktails. Fitzgerald, who at the time was on the wagon completely, tried to talk Benchley out of it. "Don't you know drinking is slow death?" said Fitzgerald. To which, Benchley took a sip and replied, "So who's in a hurry?"

....

1889–1945. Drama critic, humorist, newspaper columnist, and actor. A founding member of the Algonquin Round Table, Benchley was drama critic for *The New Yorker* for more than ten years. He wrote and acted in forty-six short films, including the Academy Award–winner *How to Sleep*.

ORANGE BLOSSOM

The Orange Blossom was the first cocktail Benchley ever tasted. Basically a Screwdriver with gin, the drink was a favorite long before vodka was king. There is a story of Zelda Fitzgerald drinking a thermos of Blossoms and getting lost on a golf course in Great Neck, but then there are a lot of stories about Zelda.

2 oz. gin
1½ oz. fresh orange juice

¼ oz. simple syrup
Orange wheel

Pour all ingredients into a cocktail shaker filled with ice cubes. Shake well. Strain into a chilled cocktail glass. Garnish with orange wheel.

From "Cocktail Hour," 1938

I MUST, MERELY AS A PASSER-BY, ASK LADIES who run tea-rooms not to put signs reading "Cocktail Hour" in the windows of their tea-shops at two o'clock in the afternoon. Two P.M. is not "cocktail hour," no matter how you look at it. The very suggestion is terrifying.

How would you like to be walking along a perfectly normal street, with the hot sun beating down on your new straw hat and a rather heavy corned-beef-hash-with-poached-egg from luncheon keeping step with you, and suddenly to look up and see, pasted on the window of a tea-shop, a sign reading "Cocktail Hour"? I am just putting the question to you as man to man.

If two P.M. is "cocktail hour" in a tea-shop, what do you suppose four-thirty P.M. is? No wonder those shops close early. By nine they would be a shambles.

"When not knitting or drinking, I often waste my time."

After drinking copious amounts of alcohol, Berryman would be seized by the desire to recite his work. Often this meant late-night phone calls to anyone who would listen, sometimes even his students. In the South of France one time, after an all-night bender, he had difficulty finding an audience. He wished to recite the "Bradstreet" poem, his master-work. As it was five o'clock on Sunday morning, he had to settle for a French baker who'd just come to work. It was quite a recital—the sun rising, the bread rising, and Berryman nearing collapse. Unfortunately, the baker did not understand English.

....

1914–1972. Poet. One of the founders of the confessional school of poetry. *The Dream Songs* **collection is considered Berryman's most important work. The first volume,** *77 Dream Songs,* **was awarded the Pulitzer Prize; the second,** *His Toy, His Dream, His Rest,* **won the National Book Award.**

BRONX COCKTAIL

The Bronx Cocktail was invented at the Waldorf Astoria by a bartender just returning from the recently opened Bronx Zoo. Apparently, he felt there was little difference between his bar and the zoo. Given the stories about Berryman, an avid gin drinker, it is easy to understand why. Too many Bronx Cocktails can turn anyone into a wild animal.

2 oz. gin	**½ oz. sweet vermouth**
½ oz. dry vermouth	**1 oz. fresh orange juice**

Pour all ingredients into a cocktail shaker filled with ice cubes. Shake well. Strain into a chilled cocktail glass.

For a sweeter version, omit the dry vermouth and increase the sweet vermouth to 1 ounce. And if you add a dash of Angostura bitters, the cocktail becomes an Income Tax Cocktail.

From "Dream Song 96," 1969

Under the table, no. That last was stunning,
that flagon had breasts. Some men grow down cursed.
Why drink so, two days running?
two months, O seasons, years, two decades running?
I answer (smiles) my question on the cuff:
Man, I been thirsty.

> "Drinking is a form of suicide where you're allowed to return to life and begin all over the next day."

One of the few writers who is perhaps as famous for his drinking as his writing, Bukowski was a puking, pissing, fighting, screwing, fall-down drunk. It's been said he could drink thirty beers in one sitting and that he could write thirty poems a week too.

There were years when he'd arrive at bars just as they were opening—five-thirty, six in the morning—and leave at closing time. The consummate barfly, Bukowski would sit on his barstool, watching. Sometimes brawling, sometimes spieling, but always writing and always drinking.

1920–1994. Poet, novelist, and short-story writer. With over fifty books that centered around drinking, gambling, and women, Bukowski established a strong cult following. His screenplay for the film *Barfly* was based in part on his life.

BOILERMAKER

....

When it comes to a no-frills beer and whiskey man, you can't get more bare-knuckles than Bukowski. The Boilermaker is quick, reliable, and easy on the bartender. Your stomach does the mixing.

**2 oz. bourbon, rye, or   8 oz. lager
blended whiskey**

Pour the whiskey into a shot glass. Pour the lager into a beer mug. Shoot back the whiskey straight and then drink the beer as chaser.

For those who like a little "frill," you can drop the entire shot glass into the beer mug and drink together.

From *Hollywood,* 1989

....

THAT BAR CAME BACK TO ME. I remembered how you could smell the urinal from wherever you sat. You needed a drink right off to counteract that. And before you went back to that urinal you needed 4 or 5. And the people of that bar, their bodies and faces and voices came back to me. I was there again. I saw the draft beer again in that thin glass flared at the top, the white foam looking at you, bubbling just a bit. The beer was green and after the first gulp, about a fourth of the glass, you inhaled, held your breath, and you were started. The morning bartender was a good man.

Truman Capote

"In this profession it's a long walk between drinks."

Capote's life was very much his own strange cocktail of celebrities, artists, and socialites. While writing the script for *Beat the Devil*, on location in Italy with director John Huston and Humphrey Bogart, he was known for his excessiveness. Capote stayed at the Hotel Palumbo in Ravello, with no electricity, no heat, and everybody "half-drunk all day and dead-drunk all night." Bogart nicknamed him "Caposy," and wrote to his wife, Lauren Bacall, "At first you can't believe him, he's so odd, and then you want to carry him around with you always." In the lobby, Capote amazingly beat Bogart in an arm-wrestling match, and then in a full-out wrestle, tripped him, fracturing Bogart's elbow and delaying the shoot.

1924–1984. Novelist, short-story writer, playwright, and screenwriter. Capote's first novel, *Other Voices, Other Rooms*, controversial because of its depiction of homosexuality, brought him wide recognition. *The Grass Harp* and his novella *Breakfast at Tiffany's*, increased his fame. With *In Cold Blood*, perhaps the first "nonfiction novel," Capote became an international star.

SCREWDRIVER

Capote called the Screwdriver, "My orange drink." As for the cocktail's real name, legend has it that an American oilman working in the Middle East found himself without a swizzle stick and used his screwdriver instead. Like the Orange Blossom, fresh squeezed orange juice is highly recommended.

> **2 oz. vodka**   **Orange slice**
> **5 oz. fresh orange juice**

Pour vodka and orange juice into a highball glass filled with ice cubes. Stir gently. Garnish with orange slice.

From "Master Misery," 1949

SYLVIA DID NOT EVEN LOOK FOR A TAXI; she wanted to walk on in the rain with the man who had been a clown. "When I was a little girl I only liked clown dolls," she told him. "My room at home was like a circus."

"I've been other things besides a clown. I have sold insurance also."

"Oh?" said Sylvia, disappointed. "And what do you do now?"

Oreilly chuckled and threw his ball especially high; after the catch his head still remained tilted upward.

"I watch the sky," he said. "There I am with my suitcase traveling through the blue. It's where you travel when you've got no place else to go. But what do I do on this planet? I have stolen, begged, and sold my dreams—all for purposes of whiskey. A man cannot travel in the blue without a bottle."

Raymond Carver

"You never start out in life with the intention of becoming a bankrupt or an alcoholic."

While teaching at the University of Iowa, Carver and John Cheever began drinking together. Soon, concerned students and teachers started having them over for dinner in an effort to make sure they ate. At the semester's end, Carver and Cheever decided to throw a big party in repayment for all the hospitality. Invitations went out, a banquet hall was rented. Before the event, however, both writers were called out of town. They agreed to meet back in Iowa City the day of the party. Unfortunately, though not surprisingly, both got drunk and missed their planes. That night the guests arrived to find an empty room—no food, no drink, no Carver, no Cheever.

....

1938–1988. Short-story writer and poet. Known for his minimalist style and his raw depictions of blue-collar life, Carver first gained acclaim with the short-story collection *Will You Please Be Quiet, Please?* He is considered a major force in revitalizing the short-story form.

BLOODY MARY

Believed to have been invented at Harry's New York Bar in Paris in the 1920s, the Bloody Mary came over to the States after Prohibition via bartender Fernand "Pete" Petoit. Pete made the drink with gin and served it under the name Red Snapper. The perfect eye-opener, it is favored by those, like Carver, who knew from a hangover.

2 oz. vodka
½ oz. lemon juice
¼ oz. Worcestershire sauce
3 dashes Tabasco sauce
¼ tsp. grated horseradish

1 pinch cracked pepper
1 pinch salt
1 pinch celery salt
Top with tomato juice
Celery stalk
Lime wedge

Pour all ingredients (except garnish and tomato juice) into a highball glass. Fill with ice cubes. Top with tomato juice, and stir. Garnish with celery stalk and lime wedge. Feel free to adjust ingredients to taste, but remember—the horseradish is essential.

From "Gazebo," 1986

DRINKING'S FUNNY. When I look back on it, all of our important decisions have been figured out when we were drinking. Even when we talked about having to cut back on our drinking, we'd be sitting at the kitchen table or out at the picnic table with a six-pack or whiskey. When we made up our minds to move down here and take this job as managers, we sat up a couple of nights drinking while we weighed the pros and cons.

I pour the last of the Teacher's into our glasses and add cubes and a spill of water.

Raymond Chandler

"I think a man ought to get drunk at least twice a year just on principle."

Paramount Studios put the movie *The Blue Dahlia* into production before Chandler had written a line of the script. Unfortunately, two weeks into shooting, he had yet to find an ending and was suffering from writer's block. He told his producer, John Houseman, that although he was a recovering alcoholic and had been sober for some time, he could only finish the script if he relapsed completely. Houseman arranged for Paramount to place six secretaries at Chandler's house around the clock. A doctor was hired to give him vitamin shots, as he rarely ate when drinking. Limousines waited outside, ready to run pages at a moment's notice. In the end he produced one of his best original scripts, and the story of his self-sacrifice became Hollywood legend.

....

1888–1959. Novelist, short-story writer, and screenwriter. Most famous for his seven novels featuring the detective Philip Marlowe. Chandler's best-known screenplays include *Double Indemnity, The Blue Dahlia,* and *Strangers on a Train.* He is considered Dashiell Hammett's principal successor.

GIMLET

It wasn't until Chandler's detective Philip Marlowe introduced the Gimlet in *The Long Goodbye* that the cocktail finally caught on in America. Surprisingly, the recipe did not use fresh lime juice. As Chandler wrote, "A real Gimlet is half gin and half Rose's Lime Juice and nothing else. It beats martinis hollow."

2 oz. gin **Lime wedge**
1 oz. Rose's Lime Juice

Pour gin and lime juice into a mixing glass filled with ice cubes. Stir well. Strain into a chilled cocktail glass. Garnish with lime wedge.

The Gimlet can also be served on the rocks in an Old-Fashioned glass.

From *The Long Goodbye*, 1953

"I LIKE BARS JUST AFTER THEY OPEN for the evening. When the air inside is still cool and clean and everything is shiny and the barkeep is giving himself that last look in the mirror to see if his tie is straight and his hair is smooth. I like the neat bottles on the bar back and the lovely shining glasses and the anticipation. I like to watch the man mix the first one of the evening and put it down on a crisp mat and put the little folded napkin beside it. I like to taste it slowly. The first quiet drink of the evening in a quiet bar— that's wonderful.

I agreed with him.

"Alcohol is like love," he said. "The first kiss is magic, the second is intimate, the third is routine. After that you take the girl's clothes off."

John Cheever

> "I love parties excessively. That's the reason I don't go to them."

When he was teaching at Boston University, Cheever found it difficult to make it through the day without a drink. More often than not, he would be rescued by fellow faculty member and tippler Anne Sexton. Sexton would spike Cheever's coffee with the whiskey she kept hidden in her purse. Such secretive drinking was not unfamiliar to Cheever, who kept liquor hidden all over his house, including a bottle behind his collection of Henry James.

1912–1982. Short-story writer and novelist. A frequent contributor to *The New Yorker*, he offered a humorous though dark vision of suburban American life. His first novel, *The Wapshot Chronicles*, won the National Book Award, and his collection *The Stories of John Cheever* was awarded the Pulitzer Prize.

RUSTY NAIL

A mellow cocktail with a lovely rusty color, the Rusty Nail
was invented in the 1960s. Touted by Hugh Hefner's *Playboy*
magazine and sipped in the suburbs, it was considered a
swinger's drink—how fitting for Cheever.

2 oz. scotch   1 oz. Drambuie

Pour scotch and Drambuie into an Old-Fashioned
glass filled with ice cubes. Stir gently.

From "The Common Day," 1978

"WE DROVE BACK TO NEW YORK after the ceremony
and your father stopped along the way at a bootlegger's and
bought a case of Scotch. It was a Saturday afternoon and there
was a football game and a lot of traffic outside Princeton. We
had that French-Canadian chauffeur, and his driving had
always made me nervous. I spoke to Ralph about it and he
said I was a fool, and five minutes later the car was upside
down. I was thrown out of the open window into a stony
field, and the first thing your father did was to look into
the luggage compartment to see what had happened to the
Scotch. There I was, bleeding to death, and he was counting
bottles."

James Gould Cozzens

"With a beer mug beside you, it's now whatever o'clock it is, and all's (for the prolonged moment) well."

Cozzens typically drank a double scotch with lunch, two doubles before dinner (poured with a heavy hand), and four beers afterward. At age sixty-seven, he was informed by his doctor that his liver was enlarged and he needed to go on the wagon. Cozzens complied, abstaining from all alcohol, even his much beloved beer. Whatever benefits this had for Cozzens's health (he lived another seven years), it unfortunately came at great expense to his work. Without drink, his creativity all but dried up and he soon stopped writing altogether.

....

1903–1978. Novelist and short-story writer. Cozzens wrote about upper-middle-class professionals whose ideals are challenged. He first gained attention when his novella *S.S. San Pedro* was awarded the Scribner's Prize. For his short story "Total Stranger" he won an O. Henry Award. His novel *Guard of Honor* was awarded the Pulitzer.

HALF AND HALF

The Half and Half is perhaps better known as a Black and Tan. The nickname is derived not just from the colors, but from the regiment of British soldiers stationed in Ireland after World War I. Called the Black and Tans, their mismatched uniforms resembled the colors of the drink. Ironically, while the soldiers were a notoriously rough lot, the Half and Half is rather smooth. An easy combination of bitter and mild, you'll find it a pleasant way to develop a taste for stout.

8 oz. chilled lager   8 oz. chilled stout

Pour lager into a chilled pint glass. Pour stout over the back of a bar spoon to help it float over the "tan." Sometimes ale is used instead of lager.

From *Ask Me Tomorrow,* 1940

WHEN HE CAME BACK he carried a stack of paper cups, a bottle of mineral water with the cork drawn, and a flask of brandy. "It's probably poison," he said, drawing the door closed and setting these things on the window ledge, "but it's bound to be warm." He separated two cups, poured an inch of brandy into one and filled the other with mineral water. "Just take a deep breath and swallow that," he said, holding them out to her. "You'll think it's summer."

"That's much too much," Miss Robertson said. Her fingers touched his as she took the cups. "You're the one who needs it," she said. "Your hands are like ice."

Shivering, Francis said, "And how!" He poured brandy in another cup and tasted it. "It's dreadful," he said truthfully, and swallowed it.

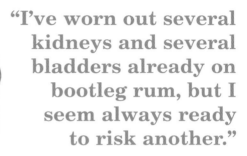

Hart Crane

> ## "I've worn out several kidneys and several bladders already on bootleg rum, but I seem always ready to risk another."

A drunk, of the complete and utterly mad variety, Crane found himself late one night drinking alone at Café Select in Paris. Loaded to the gills but not with money, Crane realized he could not cover the tab. He tried to argue his way out. Other Americans in the café offered to pay the bill, but the ill-tempered owner refused. An eager though unskilled fighter, Crane decided to punch a waiter, and then another, and then a policeman. Soon more police arrived and Crane was clubbed senseless. He was dragged feet first to the station. After a week in a rat-infested cell, Crane was fined eight hundred francs and released. He left the country shortly thereafter.

....

1899–1932. Poet. Crane's first collection, *White Buildings*, established him within the avant-garde community. His epic poem, *The Bridge*, brought wider recognition as well as a Guggenheim Fellowship. *The Broken Tower* was Crane's last and perhaps finest work.

MAI TAI

Crane once remarked, "Rum has a strange power over me, it makes me feel quite innocent—or rather, guiltless." We're not sure the Mai Tai will have that same effect on you, but it sure beats going to confession. Believed to have been invented by Victor Bergeron (Trader Vic) at his bar Hinky Dink's outside San Francisco, the Mai Tai is, at the very least, a great umbrella drink.

1 oz. light rum	½ oz. simple syrup
1 oz. dark rum	1 mint sprig
½ oz. Grand Marnier	Fresh fruit (orange slice,
1 oz. lime juice	pineapple chunk, etc.)
½ oz. orgeat (almond-flavored syrup)	

Pour all ingredients (except mint and fruit) into a cocktail shaker filled with ice cubes. Shake, and then strain into a chilled double Old-Fashioned glass filled with cracked ice. Garnish with mint sprig and fruit.

From "The River," 1930

The last bear, shot drinking in the Dakotas
Loped under wires that span the mountain stream.
Keen instruments, strung to a vast precision
Bind town to town and dream to ticking dream.
But some men take their liquor slow—and count
—Though they'll confess no rosary nor clue.

William Faulkner

"Civilization begins with distillation."

Unlike most writers, Faulkner, from the very beginning of his career, drank while he wrote. He claimed, "I usually write at night. I always keep my whiskey within reach." That he did. In Hollywood, hired by director Howard Hawks to write *Road to Glory,* Faulkner showed up to a script meeting carrying a brown paper bag. He pulled out a bottle of whiskey, but accidentally sliced his finger unscrewing the cap. If the film's producer thought the meeting was over, he was wrong. Faulkner dragged over the wastepaper basket— so he could gulp whiskey and drip blood as they hashed out the story.

....

1897–1962. Novelist, short-story writer, and screenwriter. Faulkner's southern epic, the Yoknapatawpha cycle, includes his most celebrated novels, *The Sound and the Fury, As I Lay Dying, The Light in August, The Unvanquished,* and *Absalom, Absalom!* His most famous screenplays are *The Big Sleep* and *To Have and Have Not.* In 1949, Faulkner won the Nobel Prize for Literature.

MINT JULEP

In the early 1800s, doctors used the word *julep* to describe "a kind of liquid medicine." These were remedies in which leaves from the *mentha* family were used to soften the taste of the medication. Of course, this is not to suggest the Mint Julep is good for you, but it may be what Faulkner had in mind when he said, "Isn't anythin' Ah got whiskey won't cure." He was so much an authority on the drink that the famous Musso & Frank Grill in Los Angeles let him mix his own.

7 sprigs of mint   **3 oz. bourbon**
½ oz. simple syrup

Crush 6 mint sprigs into the bottom of a chilled double Old-Fashioned glass. Pour in simple syrup and bourbon. Fill with crushed ice. Garnish with the remaining mint sprig and serve with two short straws. Sometimes a splash of club soda is added.

From *Sanctuary,* 1931

GOWAN FILLED THE GLASS LEVEL FULL and lifted it and emptied it steadily. He remembered setting the glass down carefully, then he became aware simultaneously of open air, of a chill gray freshness and an engine panting on a siding at the head of a dark string of cars, and that he was trying to tell someone that he had learned to drink like a gentleman. He was still trying to tell them, in a cramped dark place smelling of ammonia and creosote, vomiting into a receptacle.

F. Scott Fitzgerald

"**First you take a drink, then the drink takes a drink, then the drink takes you.**"

Fitzgerald's preferred liquor was gin; he believed you could not detect it on the breath (a funny notion given his remarkably low tolerance). He would get roaring drunk on very little, but then it was the Roaring Twenties, and he was the symbol. Fitzgerald and his wife, Zelda, were a pair of drunken pranksters. There are stories about how they jumped into the fountain at the Plaza Hotel, boiled party guests' watches in tomato soup, stripped at the Follies. Invited to an impromptu party, "Come as you are," he and Zelda arrived in their pajamas. Zelda soon enough removed hers and danced naked. Did anyone have to smell their breath to know?

....

1896–1940. Novelist and short-story writer. With his first novel, *This Side of Paradise*, Fitzgerald became the spokesman for the Jazz Age. *The Beautiful and the Damned* came next, followed by Fitzgerald's masterpiece, *The Great Gatsby*, considered by many the finest American novel of the twentieth century. *Tender Is the Night* was published nine years later. Fitzgerald's last novel, *The Last Tycoon*, was published posthumously.

GIN RICKEY

It is easy to imagine a warm summer evening out on the shore of Long Island—say a party at Gatsby's house, the bartenders serving up light, refreshing Gin Rickeys as the jazz band swings. In the 1920s and '30s there were any number of Rickeys (scotch, rum, applejack), but gin is the one that endured. And besides, it was Fitzgerald's favorite.

2 oz. gin	**Top with club soda**
¾ oz. lime juice	**Lime wheel**

Pour gin and lime juice into a chilled highball glass filled with ice cubes. Top with club soda, and stir gently. Garnish with lime wheel. Serve with two straws.

From *Tender Is the Night*, 1933

BY ONE O'CLOCK THE BAR WAS JAMMED; amidst the consequent mixture of voices the staff of waiters functioned, pinning down their clients to the facts of drink and money. . . .

In the confusion Abe had lost his seat; now he stood gently swaying and talking to some of the people with whom he had involved himself. . . .

Across from him the Dane and his companions had ordered luncheon. Abe did likewise but scarcely touched it. Afterwards, he just sat, happy to live in the past. The drink made past happy things contemporary with the present, as if they were still going on, contemporary even with the future as if they were about to happen again.

"**Three times I have been mistaken for a Prohibition agent, but never had any trouble clearing myself.**"

Hammett spent his later life in a famously passionate love affair with Lillian Hellman. Both heavy drinkers, their relationship was figuratively and literally on the rocks for much of thirty years. During one evening, drunk and arguing with Lillian Hellman, Hammett took the cigarette he was smoking and began to grind it out on his cheek. "What are you doing!" screamed Hellman. Hammett's answer, "Keeping myself from doing it to you."

1894–1961. Novelist and short-story writer. Drawing on his experiences as a Pinkerton, Hammett created tough heroes for hard-boiled fiction. *The Maltese Falcon,* his most famous novel, introduced the streetwise detective Sam Spade, portrayed on-screen by Humphrey Bogart. A great many of Hammett's works were adapted to film.

MARTINI

....

"I was leaning against the bar in a speakeasy on Fifty-second Street, waiting for Nora," so begins Hammett's novel *The Thin Man*. The speakeasy was the "21" Club, and the characters, Nick and Nora, were based on Hammett and Lillian Hellman. More than likely, the Martinis they enjoyed were made wet like ours. During Prohibition, the bootleg gin was of such poor quality, they needed the vermouth to cover up the bad taste.

2 oz. gin   **Olives or lemon twist**
1 oz. dry vermouth

Pour gin and dry vermouth into a mixing glass filled with ice cubes. Stir well. Strain into a chilled cock- tail glass. Garnish with olives or twist.

From *The Maltese Falcon*, 1929

"AH, MR. SPADE," he said with enthusiasm and held out a hand like a fat pink star.

Spade took the hand and smiled and said: "How do you do, Mr. Gutman?"

Holding Spade's hand, the fat man turned beside him, put his other hand to Spade's elbow, and guided him across a green rug to a green plush chair beside a table that held a siphon, some glasses and a bottle of Johnnie Walker whiskey on a tray, a box of cigars—Coronas del Ritz—two newspapers, and a small and plain yellow soapstone box.

Spade sat in the green chair. The fat man began to fill two glasses from bottle and siphon. . . .

"We begin well, sir," the fat man purred, turning with a proffered glass in his hand. "I distrust a man that says when. If he's got to be careful not to drink too much it's because he's not to be trusted when he does."

Lillian Hellman

> "Drinking made uninteresting people matter less and, late at night, matter not at all."

As far as drinking goes, it would have been difficult for anyone to go toe-to-toe (or elbow-to-elbow) with Dashiell Hammett, but Hellman certainly gave it her best. Hungover and facing the Broadway opening of *The Children's Hour*, Hellman got blind drunk on brandy. Waking early the next morning and hungover yet again, she got herself a cold beer and telephoned Hammett, who was living in Los Angeles. She reached his secretary. Two days later Hellman would realize: (1) at the time she called it was three A.M. in California, and (2) Hammett had no secretary. She took the first plane out, got drunk en route, and went directly to Hammett's house. She smashed his bar to pieces and flew back to New York. Hellman knew where to kick a man.

....

1905–1984. Playwright, memoirist, and screenwriter. Hellman received instant recognition with her first play, *The Children's Hour*. Her best-known work, *The Little Foxes*, was adapted to screen and nominated for nine Academy Awards. *An Unfinished Woman*, part of her memoir trilogy, won a National Book Award.

DAIQUIRI

Invented in Cuba, the Daiquiri comes from the small village of Daiquiri, just outside of Santiago, where the Bacardi rum distillery was founded. Nothing to do with the frozen concoctions now trumpeted, the traditional cocktail was simple and not too sweet. Hemingway liked his doubled. His good pal Hellman, who often critiqued his writing, surely took his advice when it came to cocktails.

2 oz. light rum	**¾ oz. simple syrup**
1 oz. lime juice	**Lime wheel**

Pour all ingredients into a cocktail shaker filled with ice cubes. Shake well. Strain into a chilled cocktail glass. Garnish with lime wheel.

From *Maybe: A Story,* 1980

IN THOSE DAYS THERE WAS ONLY ONE standard remedy for a hangover. My hangover had, by this time, on the wet grass, turned to shivers. I stumbled, half crawled back to my room, managed a shower, and sent for the remedy: a raw egg, a double sherry and two teaspoons of Worcestershire sauce. Then I slept for a few hours, heard the phone ringing and, several times, loud knocks on the door. When I woke up, I vomited, which is what the remedy was supposed to do if you were in good health. After you were sick the custom was to wait a while and then you drank a few beers which tasted fine and you could move for a few hours until it was time for a regular drink.

Ernest Hemingway

"A man does not exist until he is drunk."

Hemingway was not one for pretension, literary or otherwise. In a famous incident at Costello's, a New York writers' haunt, he found just the opportunity to make those feelings known. After drinking in back with friends, he passed John O'Hara at the bar. O'Hara was carrying an Irish blackthorn walking stick (shillelagh) and Hemingway began to mock him for it. Defensively, O'Hara claimed that it was "the best piece of blackthorn in New York." Hemingway immediately bet him fifty dollars that he could break it with his bare hands. Then in one swift move he smashed the walking stick against his own head, snapping it in half. The broken pieces hung over Costello's bar for many years.

....

1899–1961. Novelist and short-story writer. Hemingway was one of the principal figures of the Lost Generation. As a cub reporter for the *Kansas City Star*, he developed a minimalist style. With his second novel, *The Sun Also Rises*, he immediately became a literary star. In 1954 Hemingway was awarded the Nobel Prize for Literature.

MOJITO

Hemingway is associated with any number of cocktails, but perhaps none more so than the Mojito. The drink was invented at La Bodeguita del Medio in Havana, Cuba, where Hemingway drank them. So did Brigitte Bardot, Nat King Cole, Jimmy Durante, Erroll Flynn, and countless others.

6 fresh mint sprigs **2 oz. light rum**
1 oz. lime juice **Lime wedge**
3/4 oz. simple syrup

Crush 5 mint sprigs into the bottom of a chilled highball glass. Pour in lime juice, simple syrup, and rum. Fill glass with crushed ice. Garnish with lime wedge and remaining mint sprig. Sometimes a splash of club soda is added.

From "The Three-Day Blow," 1925

"I'M A LITTLE DRUNK NOW," Nick said.

"You aren't drunk," Bill said. . . . Bill poured the glass half full of whiskey.

"Put in your own water," he said. "There's just one more shot."

"Got any more?" Nick asked.

"There's plenty more, but Dad only likes me to drink what's open."

"Sure," said Nick.

"He says opening bottles is what makes drunkards," Bill explained.

"That's right," said Nick. He was impressed. He had never thought of that before. He always thought it was solitary drinking that made drunkards.

Chester Himes

"**Lock up a white woman and a black man in an apartment in the United States with a bottle of whiskey, and what you'll get is a violent, tragicomic story.**"

Newly arrived in Paris and thirsty from his travels, Himes and his friend Richard Wright were en route to a cocktail party when they were interrupted by a call from James Baldwin. Apparently, Baldwin, who had been publicly criticizing Wright's work, now wanted to borrow money from him. It would be a famous showdown. At Café Deux Magots, the two authors went at each other while Himes went at the bottle. After hours at the table, drunk and bored, Himes finally wobbled off. Much more interested in a piss and a pillow, he left the two greatest living African American writers to work it out on their own.

....

1909–1984. Novelist. Considered on a par with Hammett and Chandler, Himes's black detective series featuring Gravedigger Jones and Coffin Ed strongly influenced American crime writing. Largely unrecognized by American readers, he became a permanent expatriate based in Paris. *Cotton Comes to Harlem* is his most famous work.

TOM COLLINS

It may be strange for a southern writer in Paris to be drinking gin, but then Himes liked a Tom Collins. Essentially a Gin Fizz, it is a cool drink whoever and wherever you are.

2 oz. gin	**Top with club soda**
¾ oz. lemon juice	**Orange slice**
¾ oz. simple syrup	**Maraschino cherry**

Pour gin, lemon juice, and simple syrup into a cocktail shaker filled with ice cubes. Shake briefly. Strain into a chilled Collins glass filled with ice cubes. Top with club soda and stir gently. Garnish with orange slice and cherry. Serve with two straws.

From *A Rage in Harlem*, 1965

"I'M GOIN' TO HELP YOU FIND YOUR GAL, BRUZZ," he whispered confidentially. "After all, you is my twin brother."

He took a small bottle from his gown and handed it to Jackson. "Have a little taste."

Jackson shook his head.

"Go ahead and take a taste," Goldy urged irritably. "If the dead ain't already got your soul after all you done last night, you is saved. Take a good taste. We're going out and look for that stud and your gal, and you is goin' to need all the courage you can get."

James Jones

> "It is a far, far better thing than we have ever done to be disciples of Bacchus rather than of Christ."

In Paris, Jones, James Baldwin, and William Styron would gather at Jones's house and drink well into the night. On one particular evening, they decided to go out on the town. When the sun came up, Baldwin folded, but Jones and Styron kept drinking. Noon found the two writers in the Ritz Bar, still hard at it. By three o'clock, after almost twenty hours of drinking, they decided to return to Jones's place. "We went into the house," Styron recalled, "and the first thing I heard was a huge crash." Apparently, Jones's wife, Gloria, had hurled a large metal teapot at them—missing Jones's head by only an inch.

1921–1977. Novelist. Jones's most famous works were inspired by his experiences in the Pacific during World War II. *From Here to Eternity*, which won the National Book Award, centers around the Pearl Harbor attack; *Some Came Running* concerns a veteran's life after the war; and *The Thin Red Line* is about the Battle of Guadalcanal.

SINGAPORE SLING

During his tour of duty in the South Pacific, Jones undoubtedly felt worlds away from Singapore's elegant Raffles Hotel, but that is where the Singapore Sling was invented. According to lore, barman Ngiam Tong Boon was asked by visiting luminaries to create a cocktail that celebrated the natural resources of the region. The original recipe, long lost, has been replaced by countless variations, ours included.

1 ½ oz. gin	**Top with club soda**
¾ oz. Cointreau	**¼ oz. Benedictine**
1 oz. lemon juice	**½ oz. cherry brandy**
1 ½ oz. pineapple	**Orange slice**
juice	**Maraschino cherry**

Pour gin, Cointreau, lemon and pineapple juice into a cocktail shaker filled with ice cubes. Shake well. Strain into a Collins glass filled with ice cubes. Top with club soda. Drizzle in brandy, then pour Benedictine over the back of a bar spoon so as to float it on top. Garnish with orange slice and cherry. Serve with two straws.

From *From Here to Eternity,* 1957

"WHAT KIND OF DRINK DO YOU WANT, Sergeant?"

"I dont care," he said. "Any drink'll do."

"You dont want a drink," Karen Holmes said. "You dont really want a drink. What you really want is this," she said, looking down at her own body and moving her hands out sideways like a sinner at the altar. "Thats what you really want. Isnt it? Thats what you all want. All all of you ever want."

Warden felt a shiver of fear run down his spine. What the hell is this, Milton? "Yes," he said, "Thats what I really want. But I'll take a drink too," he said.

Jack Kerouac

"Don't drink to get drunk. Drink to enjoy life."

Before going on the road, Kerouac went off to sea. A young man with a thirst for adventure, he signed up for the U.S. Navy. Waiting for the qualifying exam, Kerouac ended up in Boston on a bender. He inexplicably joined the Coast Guard and then was sworn in as a marine later that same day. Realizing he was technically a member of three branches of the armed services, Kerouac did the only sensible thing—drank more. He eventually passed out at a seamen's bar and in the morning found himself on the SS Dorchester bound for Greenland. At some point in all of this he had called his parents and told them that he would be home "a little late." He was now a merchant marine, carrying a small bag of clothes and books. Although the navy would later diagnose Kerouac a "Schizoid Personality" and discharge him, he continued to drink like a seaman for the rest of his life.

....

1922–1969. Novelist and poet. Kerouac coined the term "Beat Generation" for a movement of kindred souls who wanted to break free of 1950s conventions. His best-known novel, *On the Road*, brought him instant fame, and his work went on to inspire a great many writers, including Bob Dylan, Hunter S. Thompson, and Ken Kesey.

MARGARITA

Kerouac had a great love for Mexico, for "the good old saloons of real Mexico where there were girls at a peso a dance and raw tequila." Tequila, of course, being the country's national beverage, made from the indigenous blue agave plant. "On the road!!" Kerouac wrote. "But on! Mexico calls me." One sip of a Margarita and it will be calling you too.

1½ oz. silver tequila	Coarse salt
1 oz. Cointreau	Lime wedge
½ oz. lime juice	

Rub the rim of a chilled cocktail glass with lime wedge and press into a plate of salt. Pour all ingredients into a cocktail shaker filled with ice cubes. Shake well. Strain into the cocktail glass. Garnish with lime wedge.

The Margarita can also be served on the rocks in an Old-Fashioned glass.

From *On the Road*, 1955

WHAT I NEEDED—WHAT TERRY NEEDED, TOO—was a drink, so we bought a quart of California port for thirty-five cents and went to the railroad yards to drink. We found a place where hobos had drawn up crates to sit over fires. We sat there and drank the wine. On our left were the freight cars, sad and sooty red beneath the moon; straight ahead the lights and airport pokers of Bakersfield proper; to our right a tremendous aluminum Quonset warehouse. Ah, it was a fine night, a warm night, a wine-drinking night, a moony night, and a night to hug your girl and talk and spit and be heavengoing.

Ring Lardner

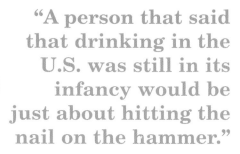

"A person that said that drinking in the U.S. was still in its infancy would be just about hitting the nail on the hammer."

A drinker's drinker, Lardner was legendary for his stamina. As a young sportswriter in Chicago, he once arrived at the paper too loaded to write. To protect his job, a co-worker put him into a taxicab and sent him home. Imagine the surprise when Lardner showed up at the office only a few hours later. Having once again toured the bars of Chicago, he was drunk out of his mind and the taxicab's meter had reached $130. Years later, at the Friar's Club in New York, Lardner would set perhaps his personal record—he drank for sixty hours straight.

....

1885–1933. Sports columnist, short-story writer, and playwright. Lardner's epistolary columns about baseball became the collection *You Know Me, Al*. His first book of short stories, *How to Write Short Stories (with Samples)*, brought him critical success. *June Moon*, a play written with George S. Kaufman, was his only Broadway hit.

MANHATTAN

A Manhattan is a Martini for whiskey drinkers, and Lardner
certainly was one. The cocktail was first served at a party at
the Manhattan Club in the 1874. Legend has it that Lady
Randolph Churchill (Winston's mother) took the first sip and
lifted her glass, toasting, "To the Manhattan."

2 oz. rye, bourbon or Canadian whiskey	**2 dashes of Angostura bitters**
1 oz. sweet vermouth	**Maraschino cherry**

Pour whiskey, vermouth, and bitters into a mixing
glass filled with ice cubes. Stir well. Strain into a
chilled cocktail glass. Garnish with cherry.

From "The Love Nest," 1926

"IS THIS REALLY SUCH WONDERFUL BOURBON? I think
I'll just take a sip of it and see what it's like. It can't hurt
me if it's so good. Do you think so, Mr. Bartlett?"

"I don't believe so."

"Well then, I'm going to taste it and if it hurts me it's
your fault."

Celia poured a whiskey glass two-thirds full and drained
it at a gulp.

"It *is* good, isn't it?" she said. "Of course I'm not much
of a judge as I don't care for whiskey and Lou won't let me
drink it. But he's raved so about this Bourbon that I did
want to see what it was like. You won't tell on me, will you,
Mr. Bartlett?"

"Not I!"

"I wonder how it would be in a high-ball. Let's you and
I have just one."

Sinclair Lewis

"What's the use of winning the Nobel Prize if it doesn't even get you into speakeasies?"

In the late 1930s, a chance meeting took place between two of the literati's most notorious nuisance drunks. This was in the bathroom of the "21" Club. At one urinal was Lewis, who was known for hurling insults and mimicry and, often, quite spontaneously passing out; at the other urinal, John O'Hara, known not for passing out but punching out. Apparently, Lewis had previously written some disparaging comments about O'Hara's *Appointment in Samarra*. Recognizing Lewis, O'Hara immediately launched into a tirade, but before it could come to blows, the Nobel Prize winner zipped up and scampered out the door.

....

1885–1951. Novelist and playwright. Lewis wrote popular satires of middle-class American life. *Main Street*, his sixth novel, brought him recognition. He was awarded the Pulitzer Prize for *Arrowsmith*, but refused the honor. In 1930, he became the first American to receive the Nobel Prize for Literature.

BELLINI

The Bellini was invented at Harry's Bar in Venice, a regular watering hole for Lewis when he was traveling abroad. Famous barman Giuseppe Cipriani came up with the cocktail during peach season. The warm hue reminded him of the paintings by fifteenth-century Italian artist Giovanni Bellini and thus the name.

2 oz. peach nectar   Champagne

Pour peach nectar into a chilled champagne flute. Fill with champagne. Stir.

Sometimes a dash of lemon juice is added. If you are fortunate enough to be using fresh white peaches instead of nectar, crush the peaches in the bottom of the glass and add a dash of simple syrup.

From *Babbitt,* 1922

THROUGH A FROTH OF MERRIMENT he brought the shining promise, the mighty tray of glasses with the cloudy yellow cocktails in the glass pitcher in the center. The men babbled, "Oh, gosh, have a look!" and "This gets me right where I live!" and "Let me at it!" But Chum Frink, a traveled man and not unused to woes, was stricken by the thought that the potion might be merely fruit-juice with a little neutral spirits. He looked timorous as Babbitt, a moist and ecstatic almoner, held out a glass, but as he tasted it he piped, "Oh, man, let me dream on! It ain't true, but don't waken me! Jus' lemme slumber!"

Jack London

> "I was always willing to drink when any one was around. I drank by myself when no one was around."

Not content to just write about adventure, London frequently courted danger, especially when drunk. Sometimes the danger was nature, as when he staggered down an Oakland wharf, made for a sloop and lost his footing. Swept along by the current, he gazed drunkenly at the gaslights of San Francisco and thought this might be the end. Muscles all but frozen and cramping, London was saved by a Greek fisherman. Other times the danger was man, as when docked in Yokohama. There, London drank sake night and day for a week, until finally the Japanese police chased him off. Forced to dive into the harbor, he swam safely back to the boat. That time he was officially registered as drowned.

1876–1916. Novelist and short-story writer. London wrote more than fifty novels. His Alaskan adventure stories brought him a wide audience and commercial success; they include *The Call of the Wild, White Fang,* and *Burning Daylight,* as well as the remarkable short story "To Build a Fire."

BACARDI COCKTAIL

Seamen love their rum. London, who was at turns an oyster pirate, deep-sea sailor, hobo, and gold prospector, seems to have had an unquenchable thirst for all drinks. This cocktail is such a lovely deep red color perhaps the old seaman's adage should be changed from red sky at night to "Bacardi Cocktail at night, sailors' delight . . . "

> **2 oz. Bacardi light rum**   **1 oz. lime juice**
> **¾ oz. grenadine**

Pour all ingredients into a cocktail shaker filled with ice cubes. Shake well. Strain into a chilled cocktail glass.

From *The Sea-Wolf,* 1904

WOLF LARSEN TOOK THE DISTRIBUTION of the whiskey off my hands, and the bottles began to make their appearance while I worked over the fresh batch of wounded men in the forecastle. I had seen whiskey drunk, such as whiskey and soda by the men of the clubs, but never as these men drank it, from pannikins and mugs, and from the bottles—great brimming drinks, each one of which was in itself a debauch. But they did not stop at one or two. They drank and drank, and ever the bottles slipped forward and they drank more.

Everybody drank; the wounded drank; Oofty-Oofty, who helped me, drank. Only Louis refrained, no more than cautiously wetting his lips with the liquor, though he joined in the revels with an abandon equal to that of most of them. It was a saturnalia. In loud voices they shouted over the day's fighting, wrangled about details, or waxed affecionate and made friends with the men whom they had fought.

Robert Lowell

> "My poem possesses and obsesses—like whiskey, that other inspirer."

Although more temperate than Jean Stafford, his first wife, Lowell still enjoyed the not infrequent binge. The only problem was that alcohol had the potential to make him drunk out of his mind (literally). One such occasion happened in Buenos Aires. In short order, he enraged the U.S. ambassador by bringing communists to dinner. He tweaked an Argentine general who, it turned out, was the country's president in waiting. He called the cultural attaché illiterate, and on the main boulevard, stripped naked and hopped onto a statue of a horse. When they finally found Lowell he was drinking and arm-wrestling with the radical Spanish poet Rafael Alberti. It took six paramedics to stuff him into a straitjacket.

....

1917–1977. Poet. A member of the confessional school. His second book, *Lord Weary's Castle,* was awarded the Pulitzer Prize. *Life Studies,* considered one of the most influential books of poetry in the twentieth century, won the National Book Award. In 1974 he won another Pulitzer, this time for *The Dolphin.*

WARD EIGHT

Named after an election district in Boston, the Ward Eight
was created at the famous Locke-Ober Café in anticipation of
another victory for the Democratic Party machine. Lowell, a
renegade from a prominent Boston Brahmin family, was a
staunch Democrat. Did he vote in the eighth ward? We do not
know. Did he drink a Ward Eight? Now that's a different story . . .

2 oz. rye or bourbon	**¾ oz. orange juice**
whiskey	**Maraschino cherry**
1 dash grenadine	**Orange slice**
½ oz. lemon juice	

Pour all ingredients into a cocktail shaker filled with
ice cubes. Shake well. Strain into a white-
wine glass filled with ice cubes. Garnish
with cherry and orange slice.

From "The Drinker," 1960

The man is killing time—there's nothing else.
No help now from the fifth of Bourbon
chucked helter-skelter into the river,
even its cork sucked under.

Stubbed before-breakfast cigarettes
burn bull's-eyes on the bedside table;
a plastic tumbler of alka seltzer
champagnes in the bathroom.

"I'm drinking hot tea and not doing much."

Not nearly so powerful as a Long Island Iced Tea, McCuller's favorite drink while writing was a mixture of hot tea and sherry that she kept in a thermos. She named the concoction "sonnie boy" and, often claiming it was only tea, would drink straight through the workday. McCullers must have felt the liquor helped her creativity. At Yaddo, the famous writers' colony, she began with a beer at the typewriter just after breakfast, then moved on to her "sonnie boy," and finished with cocktails in the evening.

1917–1967. Novelist, short-story writer, playwright, and screenwriter. McCullers achieved early acclaim with her first novel, *The Heart Is a Lonely Hunter.* After receiving a Guggenheim Fellowship, she wrote *Member of the Wedding,* another critical success; her adaptation for the stage was awarded the Drama Critics Circle Award. The novella *The Ballad of the Sad Café* is perhaps her finest work.

LONG ISLAND ICED TEA

Notorious, the Long Island Iced Tea (when made correctly) is incredibly potent, but tastes and looks like nonalcoholic tea. It's perfect for discreet drinking, which McCullers indulged in often. But be warned, invented in the Hamptons by bartender Robert Butt, the Long Island Iced Tea will knock you out cold if you're not careful.

½ oz. gin	½ oz. Cointreau
½ oz. vodka	¾ oz. lemon juice
½ oz. tequila	Top with cola
½ oz. light rum	Lemon wedge

Pour all ingredients except cola and garnish into a cocktail shaker filled with ice cubes. Shake, and then strain into a Collins glass filled with ice cubes. Add cola until color of tea. Garnish with lemon wedge. Serve with two straws.

From *The Ballad of the Sad Café*, 1951

THE WHISKY THEY DRANK THAT EVENING (two big bottles of it) is important. Otherwise, it would be hard to account for what followed. Perhaps without it there would never have been a café. For the liquor of Miss Amelia has a special quality of its own. It is clean and sharp on the tongue, but once down a man it glows inside him for a long time afterward. And that is not all. It is known that if a message is written with lemon juice on a clean sheet of paper there will be no sign of it. But if the paper is held for a moment to the fire then the letters turn brown and the meaning becomes clear. Imagine that the whisky is the fire and that the message is that which is known only in the soul of a man—then the worth of Miss Amelia's liquor can be understood.

H. L. Mencken

"I drink exactly as much as I want, and one drink more."

An ardent and vocal opponent of Prohibition, Mencken wrote letters and essays railing against the Volstead Act. In *The American Language,* he devoted pages to the etymology of bar slang. With his friends in New York, Mencken spent an inordinate amount of time searching for the perfect watering hole, the Alt Heidelburg in Union Hill, New Jersey. In Baltimore, he joined drinking clubs, such as the aptly named Stevedores, a group that "devoted itself to the unloading of schooners"— schooners of beer, that is. When not out drinking at speakeasies or clubs, Mencken was drinking at home. An avid home brewer, he once gave Sinclair Lewis a home brewery system with the hope that it would keep him off the harder stuff.

....

1880–1956. Newspaper editor, critic, journalist, and linguist. A reporter for the *Baltimore Herald,* Mencken later joined the *Baltimore Sun.* He edited the satirical magazine *Smart Set* and founded the *American Mercury.* Mencken's six-volume collection of essays, *Prejudice,* stands as a major literary achievement, as does *The American Language.*

STINGER

Created during Prohibition, the Stinger was invented to cover the taste of cheap speakeasy swill. Either you will love or hate this after-dinner drink. We are going to venture that Mencken loved it. After all, he once claimed, "I'm ombibulous. I drink every known alcoholic drink and enjoy them all."

1 ½ oz. brandy   1 ½ oz. white crème de menthe

Pour ingredients into a mixing glass filled with ice cubes. Stir well. Strain into a chilled cocktail glass.

For a dryer version, increase brandy 1/2 oz. and decrease crème de menthe 1/2 oz.

From *The Baltimore Sun,* c.1910

WHAT WOULD BECOME OF ROMANCE if there were no alcohol? Imagine a teetotaler writing *Much Ado About Nothing,* or the Fifth Symphony, or *Le Malade Imaginaire,* or *Peer Gynt,* or the Zend-Avesta, or the Declaration of Independence or any other great work of feeling and fancy! Imagine Wagner, bursting with ginger-pop, at work upon *Tristan and Isolde.* Imagine Leonardo, soaked in health drinks from Battle Creek, fashioning the unfathomable smile of Mona Lisa!

"Who cares what tripped a fallen woman?"

To pay for a holiday in Europe, Millay agreed to write some quick pieces for *Vanity Fair* under the byline Nancy Boyd. She would need liquor and company to help her get it done. Late one night, while writing and drinking bootleg gin with Edmund Wilson and the poet John Peale Bishop, a drunken Millay asked the two men to hold her in their arms. She instructed Wilson to take her lower half, Bishop the upper. Whether this resulted in a ménage à trois is not entirely clear, but it does support Millay's famous declaration, "My candle burns at both ends."

....

1892–1950. Poet and playwright. Millay was one of the most celebrated lyrical poets of her era. At age twenty, she won a scholarship to Vassar for her poem "Renascence." With her collection *The Harp-Weaver and Other Poems,* she became the first woman to win the Pulitzer Prize.

Greatly sought after in her day, Millay was known as much for her love affairs as she was for her verse. What better a cocktail then? Basically a Sidecar with rum, a Between the Sheets is the perfect nightcap. Like Millay herself, it is wonderfully seductive.

³⁄₄ **oz. brandy**	**1 oz. Cointreau**
³⁄₄ **oz. light rum**	**¹⁄₂ oz. lemon juice**

Pour all ingredients into a cocktail shaker filled with ice cubes. Shake well. Strain into a chilled cocktail glass.

From "Feast," 1923

I drank at every vine.

    The last was like the first.

I came upon no wine

    So wonderful as thirst.

I gnawed at every root.

    I ate of every plant.

I came upon no fruit

    So wonderful as want.

Feed the grape and bean

    To the vintner and the monger;

I will lie down lean

    With my thirst and my hunger.

> **"I started Thursday.
> By Saturday morning
> I'd drunk myself
> sober."**

O'Hara was a notoriously temperamental drunk. He tried at various times to punch out Robert Benchley, actor Paul Douglas, renowned neurologist Dr. Howard Fabing, and at the "21" Club, apparently once, a dwarf. The owner of the Stork Club, Sherman Billingsley instructed his staff to always seat O'Hara by the door so they could be rid of him more easily.

1905–1970. Novelist and short-story writer. O'Hara built his reputation writing about class differences. A large number of such stories appeared in *The New Yorker*. His first novel, *Appointment in Samarra*, established him as a major literary figure. *Butterfield 8*, another major success, solidified his standing. His later novel *Ten North Frederick* won the National Book Award.

PLANTER'S PUNCH

One, two, three, four, punch. Punch, which literally means five in Farsi, Hindi, and over a dozen other languages, should have a minimum of five different ingredients. O'Hara probably did not know this. Something of a barroom brawler, he believed a punch needed only five clenched fingers.

2 oz. dark rum	**1 oz. pineapple juice**
1 oz. light rum	**1 dash of grenadine**
½ oz. Grand Marnier	**2 dashes of Angostura bitters**
½ oz. simple syrup	**Maraschino cherry**
½ oz. lime juice	**Orange slice**
1 oz. orange juice	**Pineapple wedge**

Pour all ingredients (except fruit) into a cocktail shaker filled with ice cubes. Shake, and then strain into a Collins glass filled with ice cubes. Garnish with cherry, orange slice, and pineapple wedge. Serve with two straws.

From *Butterfield 8*, 1935

THE SUMMERS WERE FUN IN NEW YORK. Planters' Punches. Mint Juleps. Tom Collinses. Rickeys. You had two or three of these to usher in the season, and paid a visit or two to the beer places, and then you went back to whiskey and water. What was the use of kidding yourself? Everything was done at a moment's notice. If you wanted to go to a night club to hear Helen Morgan or Libby Holman you made the decision at midnight, you scattered to dress, met an hour later, bought a couple of bottles, and so to the night club.

Eugene O'Neill

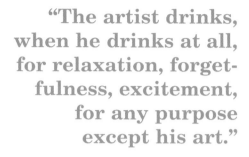

"**The artist drinks, when he drinks at all, for relaxation, forget-fulness, excitement, for any purpose except his art.**"

As a young man, O'Neill was something of a hellion. During his brief time at Princeton, he once went berserk on absinthe, destroying most of his furniture and pulling a revolver on his friend. Even more extreme were the years living above the gin mill Jimmy the Priest's, at three dollars a month. Part of a brotherhood of seamen, drifters, and wastrels, O'Neill drank raw whiskey for breakfast. Penniless, he would drink wood alcohol mixed with sarsaparilla and benzine, alcohol mixed with camphor, varnish diluted with water. Somehow it didn't kill him; in fact, decades later those experiences would help create a masterpiece, *The Iceman Cometh*.

....

1888–1953. Playwright. O'Neill's first published play, *Beyond the Horizon*, won the Pulitzer Prize; he would win three more. In 1936, he became the second American to receive the Nobel Prize for Literature. But it is his later plays that are the most enduring: *The Iceman Cometh, Moon for the Misbegotten*, and *Long Day's Journey Into Night*.

GIBSON

Whatever the original recipe, a Gibson is now nothing more than a dry Martini garnished with cocktail onions. Drinking at the bar of the Garden Hotel in New York, O'Neill often added a splash of club soda to his, but we don't recommend that. As the stories make clear, when it comes to experimenting with alcohol, O'Neill is not a man to imitate.

2½ oz. gin   **2 or 3 cocktail onions**
½ oz. dry vermouth

Pour gin and dry vermouth into a mixing glass filled with ice cubes. Stir well. Strain into a chilled cocktail glass. Garnish with cocktail onions.

From *The Iceman Cometh*, 1940

MOSHER: . . . Give him time, Harry, and he'll come out of it. I've watched many cases of almost fatal teetotalism, but they all came out of it completely cured and as drunk as ever. My opinion is the poor sap is temporarily bughouse from overwork. (*Musingly*) You can't be too careful about work. It's the deadliest habit known to science, a great physician once told me. He practiced on street corners under a torchlight. He was positively the only doctor in the world who claimed that rattlesnake oil, rubbed on the prat, would cure heart failure in three days. I remember well his saying to me, "You are naturally delicate, Ed, but if you drink a pint of bad whiskey before breakfast every evening, and never work if you can help it, you may live to a ripe old age. It's staying sober and working that cuts men off in their prime."

Dorothy Parker

"One more drink and I'd have been under the host."

Although married a number of times, Parker was chronically lonely. Her one enduring romance seems to have been with the bottle. She shared a tiny office with Algonquin pal Robert Benchley and joked, "An inch smaller and it would have been adultery," but alas the two friends were never to become romantically involved. Parker relied upon liquor and wit to combat her loneliness. Such as when she was admitted to a sanatorium and announced that she would have to leave every hour or so for a cocktail. Her doctor refused, telling her that if she did not stop drinking, she would be dead within the month. Parker's reply: "Promises, promises."

....

1893–1967 Poet, short-story writer, drama critic, playwright, and screenwriter. After working as a drama critic for *Vanity Fair*, Parker began a long association with *The New Yorker*. She was the only female founding member of the Algonquin Round Table.

CHAMPAGNE COCKTAIL

Parker, who initially did not like the taste of alcohol, started out drinking Tom Collinses. But gin made her sick, so she soon moved on to scotch and water. Later she discovered champagne. She immediately composed a poem to her new love: "Three be the things I shall never attain: Envy, content, and sufficient champagne."

1 sugar cube	**Champagne**
2 dashes of Angostura bitters	**Lemon twist**

Drop sugar cube into a chilled champagne flute and soak with bitters. Fill with champagne. Garnish with twist. Sometimes an ounce of cognac is added.

From "You Were Perfectly Fine" 1929

THE PALE YOUNG MAN EASED HIMSELF CAREFULLY into the low chair, and rolled his head to the side, so that the cool chintz comforted his cheek and temple.

"Oh, dear," he said. "Oh, dear, oh, dear, oh, dear. Oh."

The clear-eyed girl, sitting light and erect on the couch, smiled brightly at him.

"Not feeling so well today?" she said.

"Oh, I'm great," he said. "Corking, I am. Know what time I got up? Four o'clock this afternoon, sharp. I kept trying to make it, and every time I took my head off the pillow, it would roll under the bed. This isn't my head I've got on now. I think this is something that used to belong to Walt Whitman. Oh, dear, oh, dear, oh, dear."

"Do you think maybe a drink would make you feel better?"

Edgar Allan Poe

> "The desire for society comes upon me only when I have become excited by drink."

In keeping with the spirit of his work, Poe died under mysterious circumstances. On August 27, 1849, in Richmond, Virginia, Poe joined the Sons of Temperance and took a public pledge against alcohol. But only a month after, at a birthday party, he was seen taking a drink. Poe then disappeared completely, showing up several days later at Gunner's Hall in Baltimore, on Election Day. He was fall-down drunk and apparently wearing someone else's clothes. He died four days later of causes that to this day remain unclear.

....

1809–1849. Poet, short-story writer, and literary critic. Poe's first collection of short stories, *Tales of the Grotesque and Arabesque,* contains his most famous work, "The Fall of the House of Usher." With *The Murders in the Rue Morgue* and "The Purloined Letter" he created the modern detective story. As for verse, musical and mellifluous, "The Raven" brought Poe national fame. His other celebrated poems include "The Bells" and "Annabel Lee."

SAZERAC

Poe had a great affection for absinthe. Sixty-eight percent alcohol mixed with a toxic herb called wormwood, absinthe was the drink of choice for poets and artists of the mid- to late nineteenth century. Until banned in 1912, absinthe was a key ingredient of the Sazerac. One of the first cocktails created in America, the Sazerac originated in New Orleans in the early 1800s. We have replaced the absinthe with Pernod. We hope Poe will forgive us.

3 dashes of Pernod　　**3 dashes of Peychaud bitters**
2 oz. rye whiskey　　**Lemon twist**
¼ oz. simple syrup

Pour Pernod into a chilled Old-Fashioned glass. Swirl until entire inside of the glass is coated, then discard excess. Pour rye, simple syrup, and bitters into a mixing glass filled with ice cubes. Stir well. Strain into the Old-Fashioned glass (no ice). Garnish with lemon twist.

Manuscript found on the wall of the Washington
Tavern, Lowell, Massachusetts, date unknown

Fill with mingled cream and amber,

I will drain that glass again.

Such hilarious visions clamber

Through the chamber of my brain.

Quaintest thoughts, queerest fancies

Come to life and fade away.

What I care how time advances;

I am drinking ale today.

"Learn to be very stingy very soon and drink alone in the dark."

Visiting in upstate New York, Powell and Edmund Wilson drove into town one day for a bottle of vodka. On the way home, the car had a flat tire. Wilson's daughter, who was driving, waited while Powell and Wilson wandered off into a cornfield with the bottle, purportedly looking for help. As both writers were short and the summer corn tall, they soon disappeared. Hours later, Wilson's daughter returned home to find Powell and Wilson sitting on the porch. It seems they had spent the afternoon in the corn-field polishing off the vodka. They had finally stumbled out, into another county altogether, and a sheriff had driven them home.

1896–1965. Novelist, short-story writer, and playwright. One of the few female satirists of her time, Powell achieved only moderate success. Her fifth novel, *Turn, Magic Wheel*, brought some acclaim, and *A Time to Be Born* fared better. Powell was rediscovered in the late 1990s with the publica-tion of her exceptional diaries.

DUBONNET COCKTAIL

An elegant pre-dinner drink, the Dubonnet Cocktail came about during Prohibition. Given all the bathtub booze being served, the wine ingredient seems to have been just another attempt to counter the gin's harshness. As for Powell, it seems she never met a gin she didn't like.

> **1½ oz. Dubonnet Rouge**   **Lemon twist**
> **1½ oz. gin**

Pour Dubonnet and gin into a mixing glass filled with ice cubes. Stir well. Strain into a chilled cocktail glass. Garnish with lemon twist. Sometimes a dash of Angostura bitters is added.

From *Angels on Toast*, 1940

EBIE FOUND THE BOTTLE and some glasses.

"Want some?" she offered the girl.

"A half one," said the snip. "I learned that in Ireland. I went back last year, and my dad thought it was awful I didn't drink. 'Come on, Maureen,' he'd say, 'a drop'd do you good, just a half one.' He'd put away a dozen half ones. I'd say, 'Why don't you take a full one, pop, you want it,' and he'd say, 'No Maureen, I only take a half one, I'm no drunkard, my girl.'"

Anne Sexton

"I have a martini and I feel, once more, real."

After Robert Lowell's writing class at Boston University, Sexton and fellow classmate and poet Sylvia Plath would jump into Sexton's Ford and zoom off to the Ritz Carlton. Sexton would park illegally in a loading zone, reasoning that she and Plath intended to get loaded. Once at the bar, according to Sexton's letters, the two poets would sip cocktails, eat free chips, and talk at length about their first suicide attempts.

....

1928–1974. Poet. Part of the confessional school of poetry, Sexton suffered from depression and successive mental breakdowns. She found early success with her first book, *To Bedlam and Part Way Back*. Her third volume, *Live or Die*, won the Pulitzer Prize.

KIR ROYALE

Both the Kir Royale and the Kir make for a lovely afternoon drink. Certainly, Sexton appreciated the stronger stuff too (Martinis in particular). But when sitting down with a friend or a fellow poet, a light elegant cocktail must have been hard to beat.

Champagne   **Lemon twist**
¼ oz. crème de cassis

Pour champagne into a chilled champagne flute. Drizzle in cassis. Garnish with lemon twist. Be sure to go easy on the cassis, lest the black currant overwhelm the taste.

For a Kir, substitute white wine for champagne and serve in a chilled wineglass.

From "For the Year of the Insane" 1963

O Mary, tender physician,
come with powders and herbs
for I am in the center.
It is very small and the air is gray
as in a steam house.
I am handed wine as a child is given milk.
It is presented in a delicate glass
with a round bowl and a thin lip.
The wine itself is pitch-colored, musty and secret.
The glass rises on its own toward my mouth
and I notice this and understand this
only because it has happened.

Jean Stafford

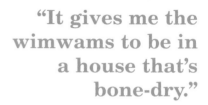

"It gives me the wimwams to be in a house that's bone-dry."

Stafford's alcohol consumption was impressive, even by the standards of her contemporaries. Often she found it necessary to hide her drinking, as she did from her first husband, Robert Lowell, no teetotaler himself. When living together in a dry village in Maine, Stafford hired the local sheriff to drive her twenty miles for rum. She used to hide bottles behind cookbooks and sneak nips from a flask she kept in her purse. One night after a party, Stafford was chauffeured home with another guest. Perhaps it was a sign of the times, but both women played sober, until without warning and quite spontaneously, they each threw up in their respective handbags.

....

1915–1979. Short-story writer and novelist. Stafford achieved early success when her first novel, *Boston Adventure,* became a best-seller. She wrote two other novels, but it was her *Collected Short Stories* that won her the Pulitzer Prize.

CUBA LIBRE

During the Spanish-American War, homesick GIs had cola
shipped to Cuba by the boatload. Legend has it that a soldier
poured cola into his rum, squeezed in some lime, and lifted the
glass, toasting, "Viva Cuba Libre." Whatever the politics, the
Cuba Libre was one of Stafford's favorite drinks.

2 oz. light rum   **3 wedges of lime**
Top with cola

Fill a chilled highball glass with ice cubes. Pour in
rum, top with cola. Squeeze in lime, tossing the
wedges in after. Stir gently. Serve with two straws.

From *In the Snowfall*, not published

PROBABLY THE PROCESS WAS GRADUAL but it seemed to
her that very suddenly and with no warning at all she was
drunk. The sensation was wholly novel and delightful. It
was an awakening to a new surrounding: the light altered,
the room expanded, the faces were familiar and her host
and hostess acquired a hospitality of which she was the
principal beneficiary. But the awakening was combined
with a delicious bodily drowsiness and though to her eyes
the barroom seemed large, to her physical being it contracted
its spaciousness into a small, snug nest.

John Steinbeck

"Only lust and gluttony are worth a darn."

Living in Hollywood, now a successful screenwriter (his script for Hitchcock's *Lifeboat* was nominated for an Academy Award), Steinbeck hobnobbed with celebrities such as Charlie Chaplin, Burgess Meredith, and Spencer Tracy. He was particularly fond of Robert Benchley. Witty, inventive, and good with a bottle, the two writers were kindred spirits. In fact, at one of Steinbeck's pool parties, they invented a game to test their capacity for booze. Empty wine bottles were placed at the bottom of the pool and various guests took turns diving down to retrieve them. If guests drowned in the process, it was decided they had had too much to drink.

1902–1968. Novelist, short-story writer, and screenwriter. Steinbeck's fourth novel, *Tortilla Flats*, brought him recognition, but it was *Of Mice and Men* that established him as a major literary figure. *The Grapes of Wrath* won the Pulitzer Prize and the National Book Award. In 1962 he was awarded the Nobel Prize for Literature.

JACK ROSE

Applejack is essentially apple brandy. Not for the snifter set, it is more raw than Calvados, and a bit lower rent. Made only in New Jersey, in Steinbeck's day it was nicknamed "Jersey Lightning." For a brandy drinker who also happened to be a champion of the working class the Jack Rose was the perfect cocktail. A beautiful pinkish-red color, the name comes from the Jacqueminot rose.

2 oz. applejack	**½ oz. simple syrup**
¾ oz. lemon juice	**¼ oz. grenadine**

Pour all ingredients into a cocktail shaker filled with ice cubes. Shake well. Strain into a chilled cocktail glass.

From *Tortilla Flats*, 1935

TWO GALLONS IS A GREAT DEAL OF WINE, even for two paisanos. Spiritually the jugs may be graduated thus: Just below the shoulder of the first bottle, serious and concentrated conversation. Two inches farther down, sweetly sad memory. Three inches more, thoughts of old and satisfactory loves. An inch, thoughts of old and bitter loves. Bottom of the first jug, general and undirected sadness. Shoulder of the second jug, black, unholy despondency. Two fingers down, a song of death or longing. A thumb, every other song each one knows. The graduations stop here, for the trail splits and there is no certainty. From this point on anything can happen.

Hunter S. Thompson

"I hate to advocate drugs, alcohol, violence, or insanity to anyone, but they've always worked for me."

Ralph Steadman, an illustrator and Thompson's longtime collaborator, put it plainly enough, "Never try to drink as much as he does." Thompson began his day with a lumberjack breakfast, never to be served before noon. Calling it his "psychic anchor," he described the meal: "four Bloody Marys, two grape-fruits, a pot of coffee, Rangoon crepes, a half-pound of either sausage, bacon or corned beef hash with diced chiles, a Spanish omelette or eggs Benedict, a quart of milk, chopped lemon for random season-ing, something like a slice of key lime pie, two margaritas and six lines of the best cocaine." It is hard to imagine chopping wood after that—or even standing up.

....

1937–2005. Journalist and novelist. Thompson's innovative writing style, dubbed "gonzo journalism," blurred the lines between author and subject. He is best known for his associ-ation with *Rolling Stone*. *Fear and Loathing in Las Vegas*, his most celebrated novel, is a cult classic.

GREYHOUND

Muhammed Ali once gave Thompson a health tip—eat a huge amount of grapefruit. Considering Thompson's alcohol and drug intake, that hardly seems a drop in the bucket. Nonetheless he took the champ's advice to heart; he just added liquor to the mix.

Make sure to use freshly squeezed grapefruit juice; Thompson always did. Indeed, he rarely was without a minimum half-dozen grapefruits and his stainless-steel bowie knife.

2 oz. vodka   **5 oz. fresh grapefruit juice**

Pour vodka and grapefruit juice into a highball glass filled with ice cubes. Stir gently.

From *Fear and Loathing in Las Vegas,* 1971

TUESDAY, 12:30 P.M. . . . BAKER, CALIFORNIA . . . Into the Ballantine Ale now, zombie drunk and nervous. I recognize this feeling: three or four days of booze, drugs, sun, no sleep and burned out adrenalin reserves—a giddy, quavering sort of high that means the crash is coming. But when? How much longer? This tension is part of the high. The possibility of physical and mental collapse is very real now. . . .

. . . but collapse is out of the question; as a solution or even a cheap alternative, it is *unacceptable.* Indeed. This is the moment of truth, that fine and fateful line between control and disaster—which is also the difference between staying loose and weird on the streets, or spending the next five years of summer mornings playing basketball in the yard at Carson City.

Jim Thompson

"An alcoholic is driven by an urge which no one but another alcoholic can understand: He must justify himself (or stop drinking)."

Thompson was one of the hardest drinkers ever to make his name in letters. Back home in Nebraska, his grandfather would pour a morning toddy down Thompson's throat to fortify him for the long cold walk to school. Later, as a hobo in Texas, Thompson would drink white lightning, home-brewed corn whiskey that could blind a man—and not just blind drunk. He drank ginger jack too, even more lethal, a ginger-based liquid sold as medicine. Still, if Thompson did not get to enjoy the fancy Sidecars he wrote about, he justified his drinking. On his deathbed, he told his wife, "Just you wait. I'll become famous after I'm dead about ten years." It didn't even take that long.

1906–1977. Pulp novelist, short-story writer, and screenwriter. Thompson was a principal figure of the second generation of hard-boiled writers. *The Killer Inside Me* is arguably his most important novel. With Stanley Kubrick he wrote the screenplays for *The Killing* and *Paths of Glory*.

SIDECAR

The Sidecar was invented in Paris during World War I and named after a French officer who would arrive at the bar in the sidecar of a chauffeur-driven motorcycle.

1½ oz. brandy	½ oz. lemon juice
1 oz. Cointreau	Lemon twist

Pour all ingredients into a cocktail shaker filled with ice cubes. Shake well. Strain into a chilled cocktail glass. Garnish with lemon twist.

From *The Grifters,* 1963

CLOSING THE MENU, she handed it back to the waiter. . . .

". . . A sidecar, say, with bourbon instead of brandy. And, Allen, no Triple Sec, please."

"Emphatically!" The waiter wrote on his pad. "We always use Cointreau in a sidecar. Now, would you like the rim of the glass sugared or plain?"

"Plain. About an ounce and a half of bourbon to an ounce of Cointreau, and a twist of lime peel instead of lemon."

"Right away, Mrs. Langtry."

"And Allen . . ."

"Yes, Mrs. Langtry?"

"I want that served in a champagne glass. . . ."

Moira watched him as he hurried away, her carefully composed features concealing an incipient snicker. Now, wasn't that something, she thought. No wonder the world was going to hell when a grown man pranced around in a monkey suit, brown-nosing dames who made a big deal out of ordering a belt of booze!

James Thurber

"One martini is all right. Two are too many, and three are not enough."

In a notorious incident at Tony Soma's speakeasy, Thurber, a fairly obnoxious drunk, tossed his drink in Lillian Hellman's face. Dashiell Hammett, pretty well lubricated himself, pushed Thurber up against the wall. In defense, Thurber tossed another glass at Hammett, but missed (he was partially blind) and hit a waiter who was cousin to the club's owner. The police were called—an extreme measure at a speakeasy. The whole event was made famous in Hellman's story "Julia" in her memoir *Pentimento*.

....

1894–1961. Humorist and cartoonist. Thurber's first book, *Is Sex Necessary?*, established him as a major comic talent. His short story "The Secret Life of Walter Mitty" created his most enduring character, while his minimalist sketches in *The New Yorker* set the standard for sophisticated cartoons.

BRANDY ALEXANDER

A girl's drink? A sissy drink? Thurber liked his brandy—as did Baldwin, Cozzens, Hellman, Lewis, Steinbeck, and Williams. Chances are, Thurber would have thrown his drink in your face just for thinking "sissy."

1 oz. brandy	**1½ oz. heavy cream**
1 oz. dark crème de cacao	**Freshly grated nutmeg**

Pour all ingredients into a cocktail shaker filled with ice cubes. Shake well. Strain into a chilled cocktail glass. Sprinkle nutmeg over top.

From "Scott in Thorns," 1962

The Drunk. He is the stranger who annoys your party as you're leaving "21." He has no name. He appears from nowhere and reels off in the direction of nothing. He talks to himself.

The Drunken Bum. Same as The Drunk, except that he asks for money, or falls down, or both. He curses.

The Souse. He drinks the way other men play cards or bet on horses. He always stands at the bar, and will not sit in a booth. He has the lowdown on everything, and loves to talk about his wife, and sports. The more he drinks the shrewder he becomes, and he is a hard man to roll, to cheat at cards, or to lure into the badger game. He could find his way home blindfolded on the darkest night of the year. He loves to sing in a male quartet.

Tennessee Williams

"Life is as much a merry tavern as a sad hotel."

If you received a phone call, "Baby, I don't know where I am. I'm at the Sheraton," then you would know Tennessee was in his cups again. In strange towns, after a night of carousing, he would forget his hotel name and insist he was at the Sheraton. His brain soaked with gin, he became certain every hotel outside of New Orleans or New York was named Sheraton. Sometimes he would ask what city he was in. As when he ended up in Indianapolis, having left for Minneapolis. He died at New York's Hotel Elysee, drunk. He tried to open a medicine bottle with his teeth and choked on the cap.

....

1911–1983. Playwright and short-story writer. Williams achieved critical success with *The Glass Menagerie*, winner of the Drama Critics Circle Award. Of his more than fifty plays, his best-known work remains *A Streetcar Named Desire*. The play was awarded the Pulitzer Prize and introduced Marlon Brando to the world. *Cat on a Hot Tin Roof* won him another Pulitzer.

RAMOS FIZZ

A Williams favorite, the Ramos Fizz hails from New Orleans, the city he so loved. Invented in the early 1900s by the Ramos Brothers, the drink is unusually difficult to make. It is not just the obscure orange flower water: you must shake the cocktail very hard for a full three minutes. At the famous Ramos bar, a platoon of muscled bartenders would shake and pass all the way down the line. For Williams, it must have been as much fun to watch it made as it was to drink it.

2 oz. gin	**1 oz. simple syrup**
1 oz. heavy cream	**5 drops orange flower water**
½ oz. lemon juice	**1 egg white**
½ oz. lime juice	**Splash of club soda**

Pour all ingredients (except club soda) into a cocktail shaker filled with ice cubes. Shake hard for three full minutes. Strain into a chilled highball glass (no ice). Add splash of club soda.

From *Cat on a Hot Tin Roof,* 1954

BIG DADDY: I sure in hell don't know what you're talking about, but it disturbs me.

BRICK: It's just a mechanical thing.

BIG DADDY: What is a mechanical thing?

BRICK: This click that I get in my head that makes me peaceful. I got to drink till I get it. It's just a mechanical thing, something like a—like a—like a—

BIG DADDY: Like a—

BRICK: Switch clicking off in my head, turning the hot light off and the cool light on and—
(*He looks up, smiling sadly.*)
—all of a sudden there's—peace!

> ## "I'm afraid that if I had a little more money, I'd decide to spend all the rest of my life drinking beer."

Words and booze, essentials to the drinking writer, were celebrated by Wilson in his remarkable "Lexicon of Prohibition." *Loaded to the muzzle, over the bay, fried to the hat, lathered, scrooched, spifflicated*— over a hundred contemporary terms for drunkenness. His was an age of "fierce protracted drinking," parties where upon midnight the guests, *slopped to the ears,* broke phonograph records over each other's heads. Wilson and his wife in fact had their own particular lexicon. In the Wilson household, currency was expressed in terms of bottles of scotch, as in "Come on, Edmund, let's have the lawn mower repaired; it's only ten bottles of Johnnie Walker."

....

1895–1972. Critic and essayist. Wilson wrote for *Vanity Fair, The New Yorker,* and *The New Republic,* but is perhaps best known for the writers he helped to launch: Dos Passos, Faulkner, Fitzgerald, Hemingway, and Nabokov. His major works include *Axel's Castle, The Wound and the Bow,* and *Patriotic Gore.*

WHITE RUSSIAN

Wilson's magnum opus, *To the Finland Station,* is a sweeping study of the Russian Revolution. Initially in praise of the Soviet Union and the revolutionary dream, Wilson soon reversed himself. We like to think it was the White Russian that did it.

1½ oz. vodka	¾ oz. heavy cream
1½ oz. coffee liqueur	

Pour first vodka and then liqueur into an Old-Fashioned glass filled with ice cubes. Stir gently. Pour the cream over the back of a bar spoon so as to float it on top.

    The White Russian can also be served straight up in a cocktail glass.

From *I Thought of Daisy,* 1953

WITH AN IMPULSE OF IRRITATION, I broke in upon the imbecile with the drums, interrupting him in a loud clear voice and inquiring whether he knew the time. "I don't know the time," he replied, with his abstracted fatuous smile. "But," he added, after a moment, when he had come to the end of a spasm of drumming, "I've got something else that's just as good!" He produced a pint flask from his back pocket: "And a darn sight better!" he added. He offered me a drink, which I accepted. I sat down on a chair beside him. "This is something," he further observed, after taking a swig himself, "that makes time unnecessary!" He had the conviction of quiet humor of a very stupid person. "If you carry a little flask," he continued, after a brief pause—he had begun softly drumming again—"you don't need to carry a watch!"

"Other men taste— I swallow the whole."

Like many a hard-drinking man, Wolfe could be his own worst enemy. One time, eager to enter his latest short novel in a *Scribner's Magazine* contest, he dashed off to see his editor, the famous Maxwell Perkins. The two men talked until the office closed and then at a bar in Grand Central Station. When Perkins's train was announced, Wolfe walked him onboard, his legs now wobbling. Wolfe talked and talked until the train started moving, at which point he raced to the door and jumped. He fell, smack on the platform, stunned. The emergency cord was pulled, while Perkins and the other passengers stared down in horror. Wolfe apparently had bruised his arm and severed a vein. It would be impossible for him to finish the novel in time for the contest.

....

1900–1938. Novelist and short-story writer. Wolfe's long and sprawling autobiographical novels were much admired by the next generation of writers, Jack Kerouac among them. *Look Homeward Angel,* his first book, brought early success. His last two novels, *The Web and the Rock* and *You Can't Go Home Again* were published posthumously.

ROB ROY

A great cocktail for scotch drinkers like Wolfe, the Rob Roy is simply a Manhattan with scotch instead of rye. It has a bit more of a bite—but then so did Wolfe. He was known to actually bite large chunks of glass out of his tumblers and chew on them.

2 oz. blended scotch	**2 dashes of Angostura bitters**
1 oz. sweet vermouth	**Maraschino cherry**

Pour scotch, vermouth, and bitters into a mixing glass filled with ice cubes. Stir well. Strain into a chilled cocktail glass. Garnish with cherry.

If made with ½ ounce of sweet vermouth and ½ ounce dry, the drink becomes an Affinity Cocktail.

From "No Door," 1934

I NEVER SAW HIM DRUNK, and yet I think that he was never sober: he was one of those men who have drunk themselves past any hope of drunkenness, who are soaked through to the bone with alcohol, saturated, tanned, weathered in it so completely that it could never be distilled out of their blood again. Yes, even in this terrible excess one felt a kind of grim control—the control of a man who is enslaved by the very thing that he controls, the control of the opium eater who cannot leave his drug but measures out his dose with a cold calculation, and finds the limit of his capacity, and stops there, day by day.

SOURCES

....

Agee, James. *A Death in the Family.* New York: McDowell, Obolensky, 1957.

Aiken, Conrad. *Collected Poems.* New York: Oxford University Press, 1970.

Altman, Billy. *Laughter's Gentle Soul: The Life of Robert Benchley.* New York: W. W. Norton, 1997.

Anderson, Sherwood. *The Sherwood Anderson Diaries: 1936–1941.* Ed. by Hilbert H. Campbell. Athens: University of Georgia Press, 1987.

————. *Winesburg, Ohio.* New York: Penguin, 1992.

Baldwin, James. *Tell Me How Long the Train's Been Gone.* New York: Dial Press, 1968.

Barnes, Djuna. *Nightwood.* New York: New Directions, 1961.

Benchley, Robert. "Cocktail Hour." *The Benchley Roundup: A Selection by Nathaniel Benchley of His Favorites.* Ed. by Nathaniel Benchley. Chicago: University of Chicago Press, 1983.

Benson, Jackson J. *The True Adventures of John Steinbeck, Writer.* New York: Viking, 1984.

Bergreen, Laurence. *James Agee: A Life.* New York: Dutton, 1984.

Berryman, John. *The Dream Songs.* New York: Farrar, Straus & Giroux, 1969.

Brinkley, Douglas. "Contentment Was Not Enough: The Final Days at Owl Farm." *Rolling Stone,* 24 Mar. 2005.

Bruccoli, Matthew J. *James Gould Cozzens: A Life Apart.* San Diego: Harcourt Brace Jovanovich, 1983.

————. *Some Sort of Epic Grandeur: The Life of F. Scott Fitzgerald.* Columbia: University of South Carolina Press, 2002.

Bukowski, Charles. *Hollywood.* Santa Rosa: Black Sparrow Press, 1989.

Capote, Truman. "Master Misery." *The Complete Stories of Truman Capote.* New York: Vintage, 2005.

————. *Too Brief a Treat: The Letters of Truman Capote.* Ed. by Gerald Clarke. New York: Vintage, 2005.

Carver, Raymond. *Where I'm Calling From: New and Selected Stories.* New York: Vintage, 1989.

Chandler, Raymond. *The Long Goodbye.* New York: Vintage Crime, 1992.

————. *Selected Letters of Raymond Chandler.* Ed. by Frank MacShane. New York: Columbia University Press, 1981.

Charters, Anne. *Kerouac: A Biography.* New York: St. Martin's Press, 1994.

Cheever, John. "The Common Day." *The Stories of John Cheever.* New York: Knopf, 1978.

Cheever, Susan. *Home Before Dark.* Boston: Houghton Mifflin, 1984.

Clark, Tom. *Jack Kerouac: A Biography.* New York: Marlowe & Company, 1984.

Clarke, Gerald. *Capote: A Biography.* New York: Simon & Schuster. 1988.

Cozzens, James Gould. *Ask Me Tomorrow.* New York: Harcourt, Brace & Company, 1940.

Crane, Hart. "The River." *Complete Poems of Hart Crane.* Ed. by Marc Simon. New York: Liveright, 1986.

————. *O My Land, My Friends: The Selected Letters of Hart Crane.* Ed. by Langdon Hammer and Brom Weber. New York: Four Walls Eight Windows, 1997.

Dabney, Lewis M. *Edmund Wilson: A Life in Literature.* New York: Farrar, Straus & Giroux, 2005.

Dardis, Tom. *The Thirsty Muse: Alcohol and the American Writer.* New York: Ticknor & Fields, 1989.

Donald, David Herbert. *Look Homeward: A Life of Thomas Wolfe.* Cambridge: Harvard University Press, 2003.

Donaldson, Scott, ed. *Conversations with John Cheever.* Jackson: University Press of Mississippi, 1987.

Estrin, Mark W., ed. *Conversations with Eugene O'Neill.* Jackson: University of Mississippi Press, 1990.

Fabre, Michel, and Robert E. Skinner, eds. *Conversations with Chester Himes.* Jackson: University Press of Mississippi, 1995.

Farr, Finis. *O'Hara: A Biography.* Boston: Little, Brown & Company, 1973.

Faulkner, William. *Sanctuary.* New York: Random House, 1931.

Field, Andrew. *Djuna: The Life and Times of Djuna Barnes.* New York: G. P. Putnam's Sons, 1983.

Fitzgerald, F. Scott. *Tender Is the Night.* New York: Scribner, 1995.

Gelb, Arthur, and Barbara Gelb. *O'Neill: Life with Monte Cristo.* New York: Applause, 2000.

Gentry, Marshall Bruce, and William L. Stull, eds. *Conversations with Raymond Carver.* Jackson: University Press of Mississippi, 1990.

Gussow, Mel. "Tennessee Williams on Art and Sex." *New York Times,* 3 Nov. 1975.

Hammett, Dashiell. *The Maltese Falcon.* New York: Vintage Crime, 1992.
————. *The Thin Man.* New York: Vintage Crime, 1992.

Hellman, Lillian. *Maybe: A Story.* Boston: Little, Brown & Company, 1980.
————. *Pentimento.* Boston: Little, Brown & Company, 1973.
————. *An Unfinished Woman.* 1969. Boston: Little, Brown & Company, 1969.

Hemingway, Ernest. *The Nick Adams Stories.* New York: Scribner, 1999.

Herring, Phillip. *Djuna: The Life and Work of Djuna Barnes.* New York: Viking, 1995.

Himes, Chester. *The Quality of Hurt: The Early Years: The Autobiography of Chester Himes.* New York: Thunder's Mouth Press, 1995.
————. *A Rage In Harlem.* New York: Vintage Crime, 1989.

Hiney, Tom. *Raymond Chandler: A Biography.* New York: Grove Press, 1999.

Hobson, Fred. *Mencken: A Life.* New York: Random House, 1994.

Johns, Bud. *The Ombibulous Mr. Mencken.* San Francisco: Synergistic Press, 1968.

Jones, James. *From Here to Eternity.* New York: Charles Scribner's Sons, 1952.
————. *To Reach Eternity: The Letters of James Jones.* Ed. by George Hendrick. New York: Random House, 1989.

Kerouac, Jack. *The Dharma Bums.* New York: Penguin, 1976.
————. *Jack Kerouac: Selected Letters: 1940–1956.* Ed. by Anne Charters. New York: Penguin, 1996.
————. *On the Road.* New York: Viking, 1957.
————. *Some of the Dharma.* New York: Viking, 1997.

Kershaw, Alex. *Jack London: A Life.* London: HarperCollins, 1997.

Lardner, Ring. *Haircut and Other Stories.* New York: Touchstone, 1991.
————. *What of It?* New York: Charles Scribner's Sons, 1925.

Levant, Oscar. *The Unimportance of Being Oscar.* New York: G. P. Putnam's Sons, 1968.

Lewis, Sinclair. *Babbitt.* New York: Harcourt, Brace & Company, 1922.

Lingeman, Richard. *Sinclair Lewis: Rebel from Main Street.* New York: Random House, 2002.

London, Jack. *John Barleycorn.* New York: Modern Library, 2001.

—. *The Sea-Wolf and Selected Stories.* New York: Signet, 1964.

Lorenz, Clarissa M. *Lorelei Two: My Life with Conrad Aiken.* Athens: University of Georgia Press, 1983.

Lowell, Robert. "The Drinker." *Selected Poems.* New York: Farrar, Straus & Giroux, 1987.

Mariani, Paul. *The Broken Tower: A Life of Hart Crane.* New York: W. W. Norton, 1999.

—. *Dream Song: The Life of John Berryman.* New York: William Morrow, 1990.

—. *Lost Puritan: A Life of Robert Lowell.* New York: W. W. Norton, 1994.

Marling, William. *Raymond Chandler.* Boston: Twayne, 1986.

McCullers, Carson. *The Ballad of the Sad Café and Other Stories.* New York: Bantam, 1971.

Meade, Marion. *Dorothy Parker: What Fresh Hell Is This?* New York: Penguin, 1989.

Mellen, Joan. *Hellman and Hammett: The Legendary Passion of Lillian Hellman and Dashiell Hammett.* New York: HarperCollins, 1996.

Meryman, Richard. *Mank: The Wit, World, and Life of Herman Mankiewicz.* New York: William Morrow, 1978.

Meyers, Jeffrey. *Hemingway: A Biography.* New York: Harper & Row, 1985.

Middlebrook, Diane Wood. *Anne Sexton: A Biography.* Boston: Houghton Mifflin, 1991.

Miles, Barry. *Charles Bukowski.* London: Virgin Books, 2005.

Millay, Edna St. Vincent. *Collected Poems.* Ed. by Norma Millay. New York: Harper & Row, 1956.

—. *Letters of Edna St. Vincent Millay.* Ed. by Allan Ross Macdougall. New York: Harper & Brothers, 1952.

Moreau, Genevieve. *The Restless Journey of James Agee.* Trans. by Miriam Kleiger. New York: William Morrow, 1977.

Morris, Willie. *James Jones: A Friendship.* Garden City, New York: Doubleday, 1978.

O'Hara, John. *Butterfield 8.* New York: Harcourt, Brace & Company, 1935.

O'Neill, Eugene. *The Iceman Cometh.* New York: Vintage, 1999.

Page, Tim. *Dawn Powell: A Biography.* New York: Henry Holt & Company, 1998.

Parini, Jay. *John Steinbeck: A Biography.* New York: Henry Holt & Company, 1995.

Parker, Dorothy. "You Were Perfectly Fine." *The New Yorker,* 23 Feb. 1929.

Perry, Paul. *Fear and Loathing: The Strange and Terrible Saga of Hunter S. Thompson.* New York: Thunder's Mouth Press, 1992.

Plimpton, George. *Truman Capote: In Which Various Friends, Enemies, Acquaintances and Detractors Recall His Turbulent Career.* New York: Doubleday, 1997.

Poe, Edgar Allan. "[Lines on Ale]," c. 1848. Accessed at www.eapoe.org/works/poems/alea.html.

Polito, Robert. *Savage Art.* New York: Knopf, 1995.

Powell, Dawn. *Angels on Toast.* South Royalton, Vermont: Steerforth Press, 1996.

Quinn, Arthur Hobson. *Edgar Allan Poe: A Critical Biography.* Baltimore: Johns Hopkins University Press, 1998.

Rader, Dotson. *Tennessee: Cry of the Heart.* Garden City, New York: Doubleday, 1985.

Roberts, David. *Jean Stafford: A Biography.* Boston: Little, Brown & Company, 1988.

Savigneau, Josyane. *Carson McCullers: A Life.* Trans. by Joan E. Howard. Boston: Houghton Mifflin, 2001.

Schorer, Mark. *Sinclair Lewis: An American Life.* New York: McGraw-Hill, 1961.

Sexton, Anne. "For the Year of the Insane." *Live or Die.* Boston: Houghton Mifflin, 1988.

————. *Anne Sexton: A Self-Portrait in Letters.* Ed. by Linda Gray Sexton and Lois Ames. Boston: Houghton Mifflin, 1977.

Silverman, Kenneth. *Edgar A. Poe: Mournful and Never-ending Remembrance.* New York: Harper Perennial, 1992.

Simpson, Eileen. *Poets in Their Youth: A Memoir.* New York: Vintage, 1983.

Spears, Ross, and Jude Cassidy, eds. *Agee: His Life Remembered.* New York: Holt, Rinehart & Winston, 1985.

Standley, Fred L., and Louis H. Pratt, eds. *Conversations with James Baldwin.* Jackson: University Press of Mississippi, 1989.

Steinbeck, John. *Tortilla Flat.* New York: Penguin, 1997.

Stull, William L., and Maureen P. Carroll, eds. *Remembering Ray: A Composite Biography of Raymond Carver.* Santa Barbara: Capra Press, 1993.

Thompson, Hunter S. "Fear and Loathing on the Campaign Trail '76: Third-rate Romance, Low-rent Rendezvous." *Rolling Stone,* 3 June 1976.

———. *Fear and Loathing in Las Vegas.* New York: Vintage, 1998.

Thompson, Jim. *The Grifters.* New York: Vintage Crime, 1993.

Thurber, James. *Credos and Curios.* New York: Harper & Row, 1962.

Tippins, Sherill. *February House.* Boston: Houghton Mifflin, 2005.

Updike, John. "A Natural Writer." *The New Yorker,* 22 Sept. 2003.

Weizmann, Daniel, ed. *Drinking with Bukowski: Recollections of the Poet Laureate of Skid Row.* New York: Thunder's Mouth Press, 2000.

Williams, Tennessee. *Cat on a Hot Tin Roof.* New York: New Directions, 2004.

Wilson, Edmund. *I Thought of Daisy.* Iowa City: University of Iowa Press, 2001.

———. "The Lexicon of Prohibition." *The American Earthquake: A Documentary of the Twenties and Thirties.* Garden City, New York: Doubleday, 1958.

Wolfe, Thomas. *No Door: The Short Novels of Thomas Wolfe.* Ed. by C. Hugh Holman. New York: Charles Scribner's Sons, 1961.

———. *The Notebooks of Thomas Wolfe.* Ed. by Richard S. Kennedy and Paschal Reeves. Vol. 1. Chapel Hill: University of North Carolina Press, 1970.

Wolff, Geoffrey. *The Art of Burning Bridges: A Life of John O'Hara.* New York: Knopf, 2003.

Yardley, Jonathan. *Ring: A Biography of Ring Lardner.* New York: Random House, 1977.

ACKNOWLEDGMENTS
....

EDWARD HEMINGWAY: I would like to thank Ryan Magyar, George Boorujy, and Michelle Zackheim for their unwavering support and invaluable criticism. Many thanks also to Charlotte Sheedy, Maira Kalman, and the New York Public Library. To Brian Gaisford for introducing me to the pleasures of the grain and the grape. And a very special thank-you to my brothers, Brendan and Sean; my sister, Vanessa; and my uncle Patrick and aunt Carol. Finally, most of all, to my mother, Valerie Hemingway, who knew long before Mark and I did that a book about writers and their drinks was a great idea—here's to you, Mums.

MARK BAILEY: I would like to thank some friends from Summit, New Jersey: Ed Beason, Andy Guida, James Klausmann, Tim Mackin, Pete Stein, and Keith Williams—and Tim Moriarty too—for the good old days. To my brother, Paul Bailey, with me from the beginning. And a special thanks to my wife, Rory. More than anyone or anything, you helped me to become a writer—as the song goes, "I could drink a case of you."

A great many people worked very hard to make this book possible. In particular, the authors would like to thank the following: Antonia Fusco, our terrific editor. Sharp, funny, and fun to work with, you made the book better and better. David Kuhn, our remarkable agent. From the initial idea to the book's publication, we could not have had a greater friend and ally. Our incredibly persistent researchers, Peggy Gormley, Tim Mackin, and Emily Schlesinger. Forty-three authors meant countless original works, biographies, memoirs, interviews, and so on. This was an investigative journey through shelves and shelves of information, and you three were just wonderful. Our consulting bartenders, Sam Ross and Toby Maloney. You have turned bartending into an art form.

We learned a huge amount from your amazing palates and your extraordinary depth of knowledge. To the whole team at Algonquin who championed the book from the beginning, especially Elisabeth Scharlatt, Ina Stern, Craig Popelars, and Michael Taeckens. Also to Barbara Balch, Hillary Byrum, Billy Kingsland, Edward Klaris, Leora Mora, and Francesca Richer, and to our lawyers, Melissa Georges, Victoria Cook, and Ned Rosenthal. And finally, thank-you to all the biographers and editors whose work we depended on— you all did the heavy lifting. We encourage readers to look through our list of sources and to dive into these fantastic articles, biographies, and collections of letters and conversations; they are the real deal.